Organic vegetables are better than not, fresh are better than frozen and frozen are better than canned. Some vegetables are more nutritious raw, others, cooked. Above all, however, what's most crucial is that we eat a whole foods plant-based diet. A regular can of chickpeas is still enormously healthier than a chicken breast, with or without skin, organic or not.

To the heroes who have dedicated their lives to promote the benefits of a plant-based lifestyle, and the impact they had on animal welfare, environment, economy, and our health, thank you.

The Easiest Plant-Based Recipe Book Ever. Everyday Vegan Cooking.
2nd Edition. Copyrights © 2018 by Saudável llc.
ISBN: 978-0-692-14662-0

You will love this food, and you will run faster, jump higher, sleep better, and you'll feel great after the meal.

Chef Fernando

fernando@easyplantbased.com

"Numerous scientific studies now confirm that a whole foods diet comprised primarily of vegetables, fruits, grains, legumes, and nuts, and without added oil, is optimal for human health, not only preventing a broad range of diseases and illnesses, but also reversing some of the most dangerous chronic conditions. This finding is of the highest importance because it communicates truth that has the power to save lives."

Nelson Campbell and Dr. T Colin Campbell - PlantPure Nation

This is not a medical book. We are not suggesting that you decide on your own to eliminate or replace medical treatment, prescriptions and/or medical advice with this lifestyle. We strongly advise you to discuss your decision to follow this lifestyle with your physician and have medical supervision as you transition into this lifestyle, especially if you have a chronic condition.

While and until your body adjusts to this lifestyle, you may lose weight.

This type of food is low-glycemic and low in sodium. People with elevated levels of glucose and with high blood pressure may experience a sudden and significant drop in their glucose and blood pressure. While, in the long run, these are positive changes, sudden and drastic variances may be dangerous and could be amplified by medications you may be taking. These sudden variances may cause you, for example, to faint or become unconscious. Discuss any symptoms with your doctor so she may decide if and when any adjustment in medication is necessary.

Contents

Easy **10**
Food sourcing **12**
Pantry **18**
Easy Veggies Seasoning 19
Sauces and Dressings - The Life of the Dish **20**
Zesty Tahini 21
Mayo 22
Tartar 23
Thousand Island 24
Caesar 25
Cilantro 26
Ranch 27
Quick Hollandaise 28
Easy Barbecue Sauce 29
Cashew Cream 30
Savory Cashew Cream 32
Basic Cashew Cheese 33
Basic Hummus 34
Balsamic Vinaigrette 36
Balsamic Gastrique 37
Ginger Sesame 38
Brown Sauce (Gravy) 39
Buffalo Sauce 40
Curry Mayo 41
Spicy Peanut 42
Red Pepper Coulis 43
Mushroom Gravy 44
Tomato Sauce – From Scratch 46
Tomato Sauce – Fixing the Store-Bought 47
Creamy Tomato Sauce 48
Mild Pesto 49
Mild Curry 50
Cauliflower Cheese Sauce 52

Mac and Cheese 52

The Basics 54
Basic Bread 54
Basic Rice 56
Mashed Potatoes 58
Black Beans 60
Lentils 62
Tofu 64

Meals 66
Fried Rice 66
Sushi Rice 68
Sushi Rolls 69
Chickpeas and Spinach 71
Risotto - old fashioned way 72
Risotto - how everybody does it 74
Risotto Cakes 75
Couscous - a great friend of a quick meal 76
Last Minute Bowl 78
Tacos 80
Veggie Curry 82
Mushroom Stroganoff 84
Shepherd's Pie 86
Pasta Primavera 88
Polenta 90
Polenta "Fries" 91
Enchiladas 92
Mexican Lasagna 94
Stuffed Cabbage 96
Gnocchi with Pesto 98
Everyday Bowl 99

Everyday Salads 100
Black Eyed Peas 100
Garden Caesar 101
Strawberries Field 102

Quinoa Tabbouleh 103
Power Grains 104
My Sweet Kale 105
Tuna Beet 106
Pesto Pasta 107
Tofu "Egg" Salad 108

Everyday Sandwiches **110**
Avocado Joy 110
Portobello 111
Easy Reuben 112
Philly "Steak" 113
Melanzana (Eggplant) 114
Fresh Veggies 115
Darn Good BLT 116
Easy Banh Mi 117
Easy Bean Burger 118
Chickpea "Tuna" Salad 120
Roasted Veggies Wrap 122

Fillings, Sides, Spreads, Bites **124**
Seitan 124
Tofu Meatball 126
Tofu Meatloaf 127
Quinoa Caviar 128
Tempeh Bacon 129
Buffalo Cauliflower Bites 130
Unbelievable Potato Salad 132
Latkes 134
Roasted Broccoli 135
Salsa 136
Guacamole 137
Stuffed Banana Peppers 138
Roasted Eggplant 140
Easy Chocolate Mousse 141

Soups **142**

Cream of Kale - Creamy Vegetable Soup	142
Leek & Potato	144
Creamy Gazpacho	145
Chili	146
Borscht	148
Coconut Mushroom Soup	150
Veggie Miso Soup	152
Pho, Udon, Ramen, and other Asian noodles	154
Ramen and Udon	155
Tofu Pho	156
Thai Coconut Noodles	157
Breakfast	**158**
Arepas *(Corn Cakes)* – Traditional	158
Arepas *(Corn Cakes)* - How I like it	159
Tofu Scramble	160
Easy Quiche	162
Spanish Tortilla	164
Grits	166
Potato Scramble	168
Everyday Cereal	170
Pancakes	171
Pancakes - Gluten Free	172
Sample Meal Plan	**175**
Essential shopping lists (plenty for at least 3 people):	177
Basic equipment	**180**
Basic techniques	**182**
Epilogue – The WFPB Journey	**185**
Baby Steps	**191**
Equivalences	**193**
So, what can I make, if I have	**194**
Acknowledgements and Credits	**202**

Easy

Too many times I heard from clients at the cafés that they would eat plant-based whole foods every day, if only it weren't so expensive, or so difficult and time-consuming to cook. I became obsessed with the idea of writing a recipe book for the everyday life: quick, simple and yet delicious meals that will keep us on the path of a healthier lifestyle. If you have a can of chickpeas, a can of corn and some oats, you have a meal.

I am a trained chef, and I've met many incredibly talented cooks and chefs, and I know for a fact that hardly any chef will regularly cook at home the complicated recipes we cook at the restaurants. Like everybody else, we don't want to spend 2 hours in the kitchen after a long day at work.

It is also a fact that a chef hardly ever gets anything perfect the first time. We make it better the next time, and the following. The day-to-day home cooking is not about perfection and doesn't have to require complicated recipes, challenging techniques and ingredients nobody has at home.

At the cafés, we have plenty of staff, ingredients, equipment, time, and planning. For us, it's not a big deal to do our recipes in multiple steps; we call it "prep". Restaurant-style recipes and cooking are unrealistic for when people are back from work on a Tuesday night.

What I incorporate at home from the restaurant style of cooking are a few principles of learned efficiency, like cooking ingredients in larger batches to be used for different future recipes, having premade sauces ready and using my oven as the preferred method of cooking. When veggies go in the oven, they don't need babysitting; just a timer, and you can do something else during those 15 minutes.

This is a cookbook about ease and practicality. These are the principles that guided our recipe selection and writing:

Naturally Delicious: enjoy the natural flavors of the veggies. When you overcook, over-season and use lots of ingredients, you can't taste the veggies anymore.

Quick: most recipes are under 30 minutes, and most can be a meal on their own.

Ingredients that people have at home: we refrained from exotic, expensive and hard to find ingredients, but there are a few items that we are suggesting that you add to your pantry, such as raw cashews, canned coconut milk, plant milk, tofu, polenta and whole wheat versions of pasta, bread, and flour.

Simple plate presentations: we find it unfair and demotivating to show you a picture that took 5 hours to compose for a recipe that we are proposing you can make in 20 minutes.

Few and flexible ingredients: so you can always find something to do with the items you have at home. Also, being flexible with the ingredients allows you to give preference to seasonal and local vegetables, which are tastier when picked ripe, and leave a reduced carbon footprint on the environment.

"One-pot" meals: it is unrealistic to expect that you will cook several different recipes for a weeknight meal.

Few-steps recipes: at restaurants, we have the luxury of prep staff and prep time. For everyday home cooking, we believe the steps should be fewer and more straightforward.

Inexpensive: The average cost of the recipes in this book is under $2.50 per serving.

Simple techniques: this book's recipes do not have fancy cuts, soufflés, emulsifications, bain marie or anything weird. Most of the prep and cooking is done with a blender, oven and basic handling of a chef's knife.

Play around: you can replace most of the veggies in the recipes with whatever is in season, or what you have at home. A base of pasta, polenta, couscous or rice will be receptive to a wide variety of veggies and sauces. Whatever you like a lot or dislike, take notes for the next time and do it your way.

Make it easy on yourself: have dressings and sauces pre-made to save time with the cooking, embrace leftovers and consider a slow cooker. If you just cook for one or 2 people, you may want to try a small convection oven/toaster. A convection oven is one with an internal fan, which helps cook faster and more evenly.

Look at our **redefined view of a glossary** at the end of this book for ideas. We thought that rather than building just another index, it would be more useful to give your ideas of what to do with the veggies you have.

Food sourcing

The best-case scenario for sourcing our food is fresh produce from local organic farms. We can get seasonal products picked when they are ripe. Also, farmers care for the land and the environment and grow crops without chemical fertilizers or pesticides. Our local farmers are our heroes and we ought to support them.

From our health's perspective, the absolute, crucial, most important factor is that we eat plants, preferably in a whole form, not very processed. Our message here is that **we must not allow the challenges of having these foods perfectly sourced derail us from the path of eating whole foods plant-based (WFPB).** The health benefit of this lifestyle is enormous compared to the standard American diet, and we will have spectacular improvements in our health **even if** we source most of our plant-based foods from canned and frozen vegetables. Two reasons many people eat a diet of processed foods, fats and animal proteins are the ease and convenience: these foods are cheap and are everywhere. Our proposal here is that we level the playing field: let us find choices of WFPB that are also easy and inexpensive. Let us not allow imperfection to discourage us; this is still worth it even if we are not 100% perfect. Positive and incremental steps are proven to be valuable, beneficial and must be encouraged and praised. Let us take away the excuses, and if we had a moment of weakness and ate something we regret, let us get back on the path; not all is lost because of some shortcomings.

Let's go through a few sourcing concepts that often confuse and intimidate people looking into the possibility of eating WFPB.

Organic crops are most often non-Genetically Modified Organisms – GMOs, but **Organic and non-GMO** do not mean the same. Organic farming includes the practice of growing plants with natural fertilizers and with natural biological and ecosystemic control of insects and parasites. GMO means the plant's DNA structure has been altered in a laboratory.

Over time, farmers have systematically selected seeds from their best crops leading to a natural genetic selection of the better tasting, higher yielding and/or best resistant plants, which is a perfectly acceptable practice. In recent decades, industrial farming has advanced the concept of improving crops by genetic manipulation. Initially, the idea seemed to offer some merit in that it brought the promise of feeding a growing global population more efficiently and less costly through stronger, more nutritious and high yielding crops. Unfortunately, in reality, big biochemical corporations developed *GMO crops that are increasingly more resistant to pesticides*, so that significantly more pesticides can be used on crops. While almost all pesticides are potentially harmful to our health, scientists have indicated that the genetic modification on some of the crops may not, by itself, pose specific danger to us. In other words, as far as we know, and lacking better research, the primary issue seems to be the pesticides, not the GMO itself.

Another matter to consider is that many small farmers use organic farming practices, but cannot afford to pay continuing fees for an Organic and Non-GMO certification, so, veggies at the farmer's market may be, for all purposes, organic, just not certified so.

While it would be ideal to consume only organic and non-GMO products, we believe that the availability or affordability challenges of such products should not prevent us from benefiting from the significant health improvements associated with a WFPB lifestyle. Do not be discouraged just because produce may not be certified organic. Keep in mind that animal products and most processed foods, even when organic, are likely to be significantly more harmful than those vegetables that have been treated with chemical fertilizers and pesticides. Also, these chemicals can be even more concentrated in animal products, given that livestock is continuously fed chemically treated plants, as well as a variety of antibiotics and growth hormones.

We also recommend that you always rinse and scrub all your vegetables thoroughly. This will not completely eliminate, but it will minimize exposure to potentially harmful chemicals.

Kale is terrific, and so is spinach, collard, broccoli, and all other cruciferous and dark leaves. What sets kale apart is its impressive amount of antioxidants. However, if you are not a big fan of kale, you will be perfectly fine eating its cousins. You will gain some nutrients and lose others, but there is no need for micromanaging your nutrition. Your body is designed to do that for you, as long as you have a diverse diet. Our point is not to get entangled in the idea that you must seek the trending *superfoods* or that you need to measure specific amounts of protein, vitamins, and minerals. Eat the trendy superfoods if you like them, or just, and more importantly, focus on a diverse range of plant-based foods you enjoy.

A raw foods lifestyle follows the principle that foods heated above 120°F become chemically altered and lose nutritional value. This is a matter where there is not enough scientific research to support one argument or the other. There are good indications that some foods are indeed more nutritious when consumed raw and that some specific nutrients, such as Vitamin C, may diminish significantly when the vegetables are cooked. At the same time, studies indicate that humans much better absorb other essential nutrients, such as beta-carotenes and other antioxidants, when the foods are cooked. We believe that this concern is also secondary; that the most essential principle is to eat plants in a diverse variety of vegetables, legumes, seeds, nuts, fruits, and leaves.

Frozen vegetables are a good and practical choice. Research has found that most vegetables, when flash-frozen at the origin, close to the farms, lose very little of their nutritional properties. Other researchers found that farmers that grow vegetables that will be shipped fresh through long distances generally picked their produce before fully ripe and before the nutrients are fully developed. For these reasons, in some cases, frozen vegetables have been found to be more nutritious than the fresh ones.

We recommend that you keep an abundant and diverse inventory of frozen vegetables in your freezer.

Canned vegetables are less than ideal than the fresh, frozen or dried ones. Three substances may be found in canned vegetables that can be harmful to human health: Bisphenol A (BPA) used to protect food from metal corrosion and bacteria, and sodium and sulfites, which are both used as preservatives. At the same time, canned vegetables are exceptionally convenient and very inexpensive. Legumes, for example, are a vital component of our plant-based diet and some beans require over an hour to be fully cooked. We suggest that you consider a diverse inventory of canned vegetables, especially those you particularly like and those that would take long to cook. They will provide you with options for your daily meals and will be a lifesaver when fresh produce have left your fridge, and ice cubes dwell solitary in the freezer.

Drain the canned vegetables into a strainer and rinse them thoroughly.

We once again reiterate that the primary goal is to eat vegetables even if they are canned.

Whole grains are what I often call the "low-hanging fruit of eating healthier". Switching from white bread, pasta, and rice to their whole grain equivalent is the easiest diet modification a person can make that will bring enormous improvement to their health. Whole grains contain more fiber, protein, vitamins, and minerals.

In addition to providing essential nutrients, whole grains help with the cleaning of the digestive system, help prevent gastrointestinal cancers, reduce fat and cholesterol in the circulation and help regulate sugar levels in the blood, reducing the risk of developing and helping control diabetes.

Tofu is an excellent product: soy products are highly nutritious and are the only plant-based foods that contain all nine essential amino acids, which are the ones not produced in our bodies. Tofu is versatile and can be used in many applications, from mayo to kebabs. Tofu is not a highly processed product.

Years ago, theories started spreading through many websites and blogs that isoflavones in soy, having a similar structure to estrogen, could cause breast cancer and a diversity of other illnesses related to hormonal imbalance. Myths also arose that soy would cause men to become effeminate or grow breasts. No credible, scientific, peer-reviewed study has reached or validated these assertions. Science currently shows that soy provides sound nutrition, as well as other health benefits, such as reported by many women going through menopause, noting that adding soy to their diets have helped them regulate hormonal spikes and the discomfort they cause.

Tofu doesn't really taste like much out of the box; but we believe that after using the ideas in this book, you will find a new best friend in it.

Tempeh is also a delightful soy product that is not highly processed and can be used in many dishes. Like tofu, basic tempeh does not have a great taste when it comes out of the package, but, with some culinary love, it can be made to be truly delicious. It is a popular choice for those who crave the taste of bacon.

Seitan is a wheat protein meat substitute, mostly consisting of gluten. It has a considerable concentration of protein but is not as complete in essential amino acids as soy. Not all WFPB advocates recommend seitan; I personally like it very much and have not found evidence against it. I am also spoiled by having access to Michael's Savory Seitan™, a brand currently available in the

Philadelphia and New Jersey area, which I find to be superior. Look for and support your local and artisanal producers of seitan, tempeh, and tofu.

Gluten is the main protein in wheat, including wheatberries, durum, faro, semolina, spelt, and graham. Rye and barley also contain gluten. It supplies eight of the nine essential amino acids, being deficient in Lysine, which can be easily found in almost all beans, nuts and seeds.

About 5% of the population present some level of sensitivity to gluten, in the form of indigestion, inflammations, aches, and pains. About 1% of the population has varying degrees of celiac disease, which is an autoimmune reaction, or intense allergy, that can be lethal or cause secondary diseases. People suffering from these conditions should be tested and medically advised.

If you do not have an allergy or sensitivity to gluten, we don't see a good scientific reason for you to avoid it. It has been part of human nutrition for at least 10,000 years and has excellent properties, especially when in the form of whole wheat or whole grain foods.

Many people believe that carbohydrates from wheat cause them to gain weight, while it is often the filling in the sandwich, or the sauce on the pasta that carries the caloric density. In other words, carbs are essential for us to feel satisfied at the end of the meal, and it's often the oils and fat in the regular mayo, cheese, sauces and hot dog and burgers that contain the excess calories.

Sugar is a processed food, therefore, we suggest using it in moderation. It is highly caloric and glycemic, and, while lacking complete scientific validation, it is believed to contribute to accelerating cancer growth. Agave and maple syrup are options produced with slightly less processing than regular sugar, but they are all chemically very similar. All factors considered, including cost, we suggest that you use a vegan raw brown sugar. Another excellent option is to replace one tablespoon of sugar with 2 ground or blended pitted dates.

1 Tablespoon
120 Calories

5 Tomatoes
120 Calories

No **oil** is a healthy food. All refined oils significantly compromise our physical performance and health, so we didn't add it to the recipes in this book. If using a bit of oil in any or all of our recipes is important for you to enjoy your meals and stay on the plant-based path, we suggest that you use little of it, less than you are used to, and choose the oil based the flavor that will encourage you to eat vegetables with pleasure. For example, once you see the price tag on a bottle of a very fine extra virgin truffled olive oil, you will be encouraged to use it sparsely. From a chemical standpoint, all oils are very similar, and the health impact difference of one over another is marginal. The major difference is their heat resistance in releasing free-radicals of oxygen when deep-frying, but we are definitely encouraging you to give up frying.

Alcohol in moderation. A little red wine might possibly have beneficial properties. More importantly, though, we believe a meal should be pleasurable; if you enjoy a glass of wine and no medical condition prevents you, go for it.

Commercial veggie burgers, mock chicken, and mock meat patties are usually very processed and often contain limited nutrients and excessive oils, sugar, sodium, and preservatives, and cannot generally be considered a whole food, even if they are plant-based. At the same time, veggie burgers and other such items are very convenient. We encourage you to read the labels and pick the ones with fewer added chemicals and processed ingredients.

Our general recommendation is to avoid products that are not WFPB, but we, yet once more, want to reiterate our philosophy of not allowing a strive for perfection to discourage your efforts to live the plant-based lifestyle. We sincerely understand that once in a while you may crave a mock chicken nugget or want to add vegan cheese or a commercial vegan mayo to your meal. We believe that it is a more productive approach to allow ourselves an occasional indulgence than to abandon the path to WFPB because of the perception that the bar is set too high and we can't possibly reach it.

Pantry

What should a person realistically have at home? I do a lot of cooking at the restaurant and, except for special occasions, the meals I prepare at home are quick and easy, and that matches what I stock in my home pantry, fridge, and freezer:

Fresh:

- Vegetables: tomato, peppers, cucumber, carrot, celery, onion, potatoes, garlic, spinach, kale, cauliflower, broccoli, and mushroom.

- Herbs: cilantro, parsley, green onions, and basil.
- Extra firm regular tofu and extra firm silken tofu.

Dried:

- Legumes: lentils, beans of different varieties, and chickpeas.
- Brown Basmati rice, my favorite brown rice.
- Raisins and dates.
- Oats: old-fashioned, or rolled oats are beautifully practical if you are in a hurry and want to add a nutritious and fiber-rich starch component to your meal that needs little to no cooking. If you cooked beans and ran out of rice, just pour the beans over the oats, and voilà. Steel cut oats are great for hot cereal bowls.
- Whole-wheat pasta (I like fusilli) and whole-wheat couscous.
- Polenta and/or grits.
- Multigrain hot cereal, for breakfast.

Frozen:

- Corn, peas, spinach, edamame, kale, broccoli, and cauliflower. Also fruit for my wife's smoothies.

Canned:

- Chickpeas, black eye peas, beans of many varieties, palm hearts, and coconut milk.

Some veggies, more than others, suffer a lot in taste when canned. As much as possible and practical, you may want to go for the fresh or frozen version of them. You can cook all these veggies relatively fast and avoid the tasteless and overcooked canned equivalent: peas, asparagus, string beans, spinach, collard greens, carrots, potatoes, and beets.

Bottled or Jarred:
- Tomato sauce and tomato juice
- Carton soy, cashew, almond or coconut milk.
- Capers, olives, pickles, and relish.
- Peanut butter and tahini paste.
- Lemon juice.

Nuts:
- Raw cashews (broken raw cashews can be found at Asian stores at more reasonable prices) and sesame seeds.
- Roasted walnuts, almonds or peanuts, for snacks or toppings.

Seasonings:
- Dijon mustard, ketchup, rice, and balsamic vinegar, soy sauce, hot sauce, and raw sugar. Salt, curry powder, cumin, coriander, garlic powder, lemon pepper, old bay, paprika, turmeric, nutmeg, and cinnamon.

At the restaurant, we make a few of our own spice mixes to simplify the seasoning of vegetables and recipes. Here's one combination that is versatile and can be used to season almost anything:

Easy Veggies Seasoning

1 part Old Bay® or similar
1 part lemon pepper
1 part garlic powder
2 parts salt

At the restaurant, "1 part" means 1 quart; at home, 1 part can be a tablespoon or a ¼ cup. Mix well and keep it in a jar or shaker to sprinkle on the veggies for roasting, or add it anywhere you like. I prefer to use this season before the cooking, so the garlic powder rehydrates. You may replace the Old Bay® with any of your preferred seasoning mixes, like Mexican, Jerk or Cajun.

Sauces and Dressings - The Life of the Dish

Always having a sauce or dressing readily available will save you half the time for getting your meal ready to serve. I often just look for a recipe that works with the sauce or sauce ingredients I have.

Zesty Tahini

Thousand Island

Cilantro

Mayo

Tartar

Ginger Sesame

Zesty Tahini

 10 minutes    12 oz

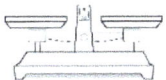
½ cup tahini paste
1 cup water
2 Tablespoons lemon juice or vinegar
2 garlic cloves
1 teaspoon salt

This is an effortless and versatile creamy dressing. It can be used for hot or cold dishes; also works well as a mayo substitute (if that is your plan, increase tahini to ¾ cup). Some people find the taste of tahini a bit bitter and prefer to add more water and make this sauce a bit runnier so that the bitterness is milder. Another option is to add a bit more water along with add 1-2 tablespoons of cornstarch, to make it thicker again, but with less tahini.

Add all ingredients to the blender and blend well, until very smooth. This ratio should make a thick sauce, but the thickness of tahini pastes vary, as well as the thickness of the paste on top vs. the bottom of the jar (give the jar a vigorous shake before you open it). If too thick, add more water in small increments. It will get some 10% thicker as it chills in the fridge.

Other ingredient options:

- caper/olives brine can replace lemon juice adding a delicious flavor
- a tablespoon of Dijon mustard adds an enhanced flavor
- add your preferred hot sauce
- use orange, or other fruit juice instead of water for a sweeter version
- add your favorite herb or spice, such as cilantro, parsley, rosemary, thyme or basil
- Can't find tahini? You can use peanut butter or almond butter.

Shiish! Too runny: blend in a bit more tahini; or if too salty, add tahini and water. If you are out of tahini, you may use a piece of tofu, or a few raw cashews or peanut butter, or a bit of thickener, such as cornstarch.

Nice touch: roasting the garlic will give a deeper flavor.

Mayo

 10 minutes  1 Pint

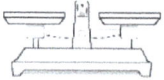
1 pack of silken tofu
0 to ½ cup water (depends on the tofu)
1 Tablespoon lemon juice or vinegar
1-2 Tablespoons Dijon mustard
1-2 teaspoons salt
1-3 cloves garlic
1 Tablespoon cornstarch
½ teaspoon sugar

This is a tasty oil-free mayo. Add more Dijon and garlic for a bolder flavor.

The silken tofu makes a difference; regular tofu works but has a stronger flavor with a bit of an after-taste. You may soften this aftertaste adding a few cashews, more lemon juice, mustard, and/or garlic.

The reason for adding cornstarch is that it's challenging to blend tofu with little water for the right mayo consistency, as the paste will tend to float above the blender blade. We are making it a bit runnier, then letting the thickener do its job once you refrigerate the Mayo.

Add all ingredients to the blender and blend well, until very smooth. Some silken tofu will require no water for this mix to blend, while other firmer tofu may require up to ½ cup of water; add as little as necessary to blend. The goal is to keep it as thick as possible, and yet blendable.

Other Ingredients:

- caper/olives brine can replace lemon juice adding a delicious flavor
- any mustard works, I just like the taste of Dijon better
- a pinch of turmeric (good anti-inflammatory) and/or hot sauce for color and flavor.

Shiish! Too runny: blend in a bit more tofu, or if too salty, add more tofu and water. If you are out of tofu, you may use raw cashews or tahini, or more thickener, such as cornstarch.

Tartar

 10 minutes  1 Pint

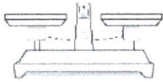
1 pack of silken tofu
0 to ½ cup water (depends on the tofu)
1 Tablespoon lemon juice or vinegar
1-2 Tablespoons Dijon mustard
1-2 teaspoons salt
1-3 cloves garlic
1 Tablespoon cornstarch
½ teaspoon sugar
¼ cup relish
¼ to ½ of a small onion
1 Tablespoon capers (optional)

This tastes great with a veggie burger *(page 116)*, or for dipping pretty much anything in it.

If you already have 1 pint of Mayo *(page 22)*, just add the minced onions, relish, and caper, and perhaps a bit more Dijon mustard, to your taste.

Add all ingredients to the blender except the relish, onion, and capers, and blend well, until very smooth.

Some silken tofu will require no water for this mix to blend, while other firmer tofu may require up to ½ cup of water; add as little as necessary to blend. The goal is to keep it as thick as possible, and yet blendable.

Remove from the blender and add relish, and minced onion and capers.

Thousand Island

 10 minutes    1 Pint

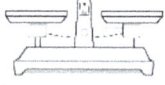
1 pack of silken tofu
¼ to ½ cup water (depends on the tofu)
1 Tablespoon lemon juice or vinegar
1-2 Tablespoons Dijon mustard
1-2 teaspoons salt
1-3 cloves garlic
1 Tablespoon cornstarch
2 teaspoons sugar
½ cup of a thick tomato sauce or tomato puree
1 teaspoon paprika
¼ cup relish
¼ to ½ of a small onion
pinch of dill

This is another favorite for sandwiches and salads. Trivia has many versions for its origin, referring to the Thousand Islands region at the Northeast corner of lake Ontario between the USA and Canada, where either this dressing was first improvised or is the origin of the person who first improvised it. The archipelago has, in fact, closer to two thousand islands.

If you already have 1 pint of Mayo *(page 22)*, just add tomato sauce, paprika relish, onion, sugar, and dill.

 Add all ingredients except relish, onions, and dill to the blender and blend well, until very smooth.

Some silken tofu will require no water for this mix to blend, while other firmer tofu may require up to ½ cup of water; add as little as necessary to blend. The goal is to keep it as thick as possible, and yet blendable.

Remove from the blender and add dill, relish and minced onions.

Shortcut: you may use ketchup, instead of the tomato sauce and sugar.

Caesar

 10 minutes    1 Pint

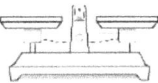
1 pack silken tofu
0 to ½ cup water (depends on the tofu)
1 Tablespoon lemon juice or vinegar
1-2 Tablespoons Dijon mustard
1 teaspoon salt
1-3 cloves garlic
1 Tablespoon cornstarch
½ teaspoon sugar
1 teaspoon onion powder
1 Tablespoon vegan Worcestershire or soy sauce
1 Tablespoon miso (optional)
1 Tablespoon nutritional yeast (optional)
½ cup capers

Caesar gained a bad name for being terribly caloric, and people gave up on it. Now you have a chance to enjoy it back, and it tastes pretty close to "regular" Caesar.

If you already have 1 pint of Mayo *(page 22)*, just add the last 5 ingredients and one extra garlic clove.

 Add all ingredients except capers to the blender and blend well, until very smooth.

Some silken tofu will require no water for this mix to blend, while other firmer tofu may require up to ½ cup of water; add as little as necessary to blend. The goal is to keep it as thick as possible, and yet blendable.

Add capers after the sauce is ready; chop them by hand or blend at medium-low speed for a few seconds, just enough to mince, but not liquefy.

If you like it a bit tarter, add 1-2 more Tablespoons of vinegar or lemon juice.

Cilantro

 10 minutes  1 Pint

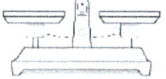
1 pack of silken tofu
0 to ½ cup water (depends on the tofu)
1 Tablespoon lemon juice or vinegar
2 Tablespoons Dijon mustard
1-2 teaspoons salt
2-4 cloves garlic
1 Tablespoon cornstarch
½ teaspoon sugar
½ bunch cilantro

I absolutely love this dressing; it works wonders for sandwiches like a Banh Mi *(page 117)* or as a light dressing for salads and bowls.

Some people hate cilantro; it tastes like soap to them. It is estimated that some 5% of the population, mostly from northern European heritage, have taste buds that are adversely sensitive to cilantro. If that's your case, You may try this with parsley, basil or just spinach.

If you already have 1 pint of Mayo *(page 22)*, just add the ½ bunch of cilantro, another 1-2 cloves of garlic and a tablespoon of mustard.

Add all ingredients to the blender and blend well, until very smooth.

Some silken tofu will require no water for this mix to blend, while other firmer tofu may require up to ½ cup of water; add as little as necessary to blend. The goal is to keep it as thick as possible, and yet blendable.

Ranch

 10 minutes    1 Pint

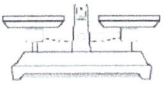
1 pack silken tofu
2 Tablespoons to ¼ to cup water (depends on the tofu)
1 Tablespoon lemon juice
1-2 Tablespoons Dijon mustard
1-2 teaspoons salt
1-3 cloves garlic
1 Tablespoon cornstarch
½ teaspoon sugar
1 teaspoon onion powder
1 teaspoon ginger powder
1 Tablespoon nutritional yeast
¼ cup vinegar
6 sprigs parsley
1 Tablespoon dill

Ranch dressing

I like this one better on salads or as a dip, but I've used it on sandwiches and wraps. If you already have 1 pint of Mayo *(page 22)*, just add the last 6 ingredients, and, if needed, a tablespoon of corn starch.

Add all ingredients except parsley and dill to the blender and blend well, until very smooth.

Some silken tofu will require no water for this mix to blend, while other firmer tofu may require up to ½ cup of water; add as little as necessary to blend. The goal is to keep it as thick as possible, and yet blendable.

Add parsley and dill after the sauce is ready and blend at medium-low speed for about 30 seconds, just enough to mince, but not liquefy.

Quick Hollandaise

 10 minutes  1 Cup

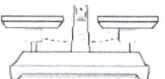
1 cup Mayo *(page 22)*
2 Tablespoons water
¼ teaspoon turmeric
¼ teaspoon paprika
½ teaspoon lemon juice or vinegar
A good drizzle of hot sauce
Salt, if you believe it needs more

I like to add this sauce to my tofu scramble or pour on roasted veggies.

Hollandaise

Add all ingredients to a small pot, turn the heat to medium and stir with a whisk, spatula or non-scratching spoon until warm. No need to boil; it is okay if it does, but will start to stick to the bottom. Add more water as necessary.

Easy Barbecue Sauce

 10 minutes    1 ½ Pint

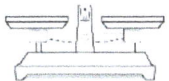

1 onion
2 cloves garlic
1 pint of tomato sauce
1 teaspoon salt
½ cup raw sugar
½ cup vinegar
1 Tablespoon mustard
2 Tablespoon soy sauce or tamari
1-3 Tablespoons hot sauce (optional)
1 teaspoon paprika (optional)
5-10 drops liquid smoke (optional)

Easy Barbecue Sauce

 Heat a pan or pot on medium-high. Cut the onions and garlic in any shape you like (if you will blend) or in neat fine dicing and mince, if you prefer your BBQ chunky, then roast it until nicely browned. Add all other ingredients, bring to boil, and simmer for about 5 minutes.

At this point, it's ready to be blended and used in any way you like. If you prefer your BBQ chunky; cook a little longer, and the onions will gradually  shrink and even dissolve. You may simmer it longer, as much as 2 hours, to bring up sweetness and deeper color, and to make the foam from the blending disappear.

Other ingredients: to make it even easier, you may use ketchup instead of the tomato sauce, and you may use garlic and onion powders, instead of fresh ones. There are millions of BBQ recipes out there, using fruit such as peaches for sweetening and a diversity of spices, hot peppers, bourbons and herbs that go way beyond the scope of this book, but barbecues are fun to research and play with, so we encourage you to add ingredients and play around.

Cashew Cream

 10 minutes    12 oz

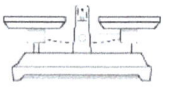   **1 cup raw cashews**
1 cup water

Trivia: Cashews are the seed of the cashew fruit.

They are a creamier and smoother nut that is easy to blend and makes a very versatile cream with a mild flavor.

This is an excellent replacement for every recipe that uses heavy cream or sour cream (add 1 tablespoon of vinegar).

If you are allergic to cashews or can't find them, your next best option is canned coconut milk. It works just as well, but it brings a bit more flavor, which may either complement or interfere with the flavors of your recipe. Another option is to just blend tofu, in approximately the same 1:1 ratio with water.

 If you have a strong blender, you don't need to soak the cashews; otherwise, soak the cashews for 15-30 minutes before blending, to soften them.

Add cashew and water to the blender and blend without mercy, for several minutes, until very smooth.

When you use it for further cooking, it will get thicker, and you may need to add water to the pot.

Shiish! I bought roasted cashews! It will work, just will taste a bit different, for the roasting flavor. Let it soak for about one hour, then blend.

Variations: mix or replace all or some of the cashews with white beans, for a leaner cream

Triple or quadruple the water for cashew milk. Let it blend for a long time, but don't burn your motor. A strong blender will run for 3-5 minutes with no stress, other blenders will recommend that you give it a break, after one minute. You want to make sure there are no solid residues. To be sure, you may strain it through a fine mesh strainer or a cheesecloth or gaze.

Double or triple the water for a coffee creamer. If you like, add sweetener, vanilla, nutmeg, chocolate, cinnamon and/or other flavorings of your choice.

Savory Cashew Cream

 10 minutes   12 oz

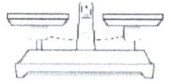
1 cup raw cashews
1 cup water
1-3 garlic cloves
1 teaspoon lemon juice (or vinegar)
1-2 teaspoon Dijon mustard (or any other mustard)
1 teaspoon salt
1 teaspoon nutritional yeast (optional, for flavor)

This is a very versatile base sauce and a quick-and-easy sauce for pasta (add tomato sauce or paste for a creamy tomato pasta sauce). Can also be a foundation for a mushroom gravy, a veggies casserole or even curries.

If you have a strong blender, you don't need to soak the cashews; otherwise, soak the cashew for 30 minutes before blending.

Add all ingredients to the blender and blend the living daylights out of it, for several minutes, until very smooth.

When you use it for further cooking, it will get thicker in the pot, and you may need to add water to adjust the consistency.

Other Ingredient options:
- Replace some or all of the cashews with white beans, for a leaner cream
- Replacing the mustard with miso works fine.
- If you make it thicker, by reducing the water or increasing cashews, it will work as a spread
- ¼ teaspoon of turmeric and paprika for a cheddar style coloring
- 1 cup of tomato sauce or ¼ cup of tomato paste for a creamy tomato sauce for pasta
- 1 Tablespoon of curry powder or paste for a basic curry sauce

Shiish! I bought roasted cashews! It will work, just will taste a bit different, for the roasting flavor. Let it soak for about one hour, then blend.

Basic Cashew Cheese

 20 minutes 8 oz

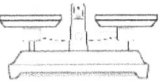
1 cup raw cashews
1 cup water
1 garlic clove
1 teaspoon nutritional yeast
1 teaspoon lemon juice
1 teaspoon Dijon mustard
1 teaspoon salt
2 teaspoons tapioca
2 Tablespoons agar-agar powder (sorry!)

This recipe is as simple as possible for a vegan cheese; it has the creamy, tart, salty, bitter and firming elements. If you get into it, the book "Artisan Vegan Cheese", by Miyoko Schinner, really takes it to the next level. Miyoko uses a fermentation process called rejuvelac, which brings a tart flavor that cannot be matched by lemon juice or vinegar.

Add all ingredients to the blender and blend well, for several minutes, until very smooth.

Pour the blended cream into a medium pot, whisk or stir as it simmers, until it thickens to a very thick paste, about 10 minutes. The agar-agar is a natural vegan gelatin obtained from  an alga, and, like regular gelatin, will activate when it chills.

Move to a mold and let it chill overnight. Remove from the mold and enjoy.

Basic Hummus

 15 minutes    1 Pint

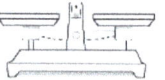
1 can chickpeas
¼ to ½ cup Tahini
1 teaspoon salt (adjust to taste)
2 Tablespoons lemon juice
¼ to ½ cup water (start with ¼)
2-3 garlic cloves
½ teaspoon cumin
½ teaspoon coriander
½ teaspoon of raw sugar

Hummus is a staple. Many middle-eastern and Mediterranean countries claim to be the inventor and perfector of hummus, as well as the flat breads that often accompany it. The word itself is Arabic, but Israelis hold it as a national treasure. You will find many variations, each stating to be the original and best. I'm sure you will develop your own variation that will rise to the top. Hummus is delicious and very versatile: it can be a dressing or a dip, or a replacement for mayo that goes with any sandwich or wrap.

Basic Hummus with olives and capers

 Add all ingredients to the blender or processor. Most blenders will work better than most processors.

Blend or mix well, for a long time, adding more water if necessary. It will get some 10-20% thicker after chilling in the fridge.

I am not a fan because I believe it affects the taste, but some people claim the chickpea can brine (aquafaba) makes a smoother hummus; the amount of brine in one can of chickpeas may be too much liquid, so, strain it to a cup and add it as if it were the water from the recipe.

Other ingredient options:
- adding chopped parsley is a classic; adding chopped green onions along with parsley makes it even better. I've seen it made with cilantro, by accident, and I happened to like it.
- I love adding capers or olives; about ¼ to ½ cup. You may use the brine to replace the lemon juice and reduce or eliminate the salt. For a rustic finish, chop the olives by hand, so the hummus will show olive chunks, instead of adding them to the blender.
- add a splash of your preferred hot sauce
- a roasted red pepper or a few beet slices for a red flare
- ¼ bunch of basil, 2 more garlic cloves and ¼ cup of chopped nuts for a pesto style
- hummus can be made with any bean, like fava beans, instead of chickpeas.

***

UNLIMITED VARIATIONS

Shiish! Too runny, or too salty: Blend more chickpeas and/or tahini. You may also use a piece of tofu, a few raw cashews or even peanut butter, or a bit of thickener such as cornstarch.

Nice Touch: if you have time to soak and cook dried chickpeas, instead of using a can, it will taste significantly better. For the proportion of this recipe, you will need ~ ¾ cup of dried chickpeas.

Balsamic Vinaigrette

 10 minutes  12 oz

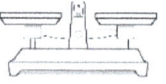
1 cup water
~½ cup Balsamic vinegar
1 Tablespoon mustard
2 garlic cloves
1 teaspoon salt (adjust to taste)
1 cup Raisins
A drizzle of hot sauce or a pinch of black pepper
3 sprigs of Parsley (optional)
Salt if you believe it necessary

Most balsamic vinaigrette dressings are 80% oil. This recipe will make a creamy and delicious dressing for less than half of the calories.

 Add all ingredients except the parsley to a blender and blend well. Add parsley at the end, at a slower speed and just for a brief moment, so to mince but not to entirely blend it.

It will get some 20% thicker after you refrigerate, and the foamy looks will settle to a darker dressing.

Balsamic Gastrique

 15 minutes

Balsamic gastrique, glaze or reduction is done by simply simmering balsamic vinegar. It results in a sweet glaze that has the deliciousness of balsamic vinegar, with much less acidity.

The quality of the balsamic vinegar directly, and significantly impacts the quality and thickness of the reduction.

 Add the balsamic vinegar to a small pot, in any quantity. Bring to boil, then reduce the heat to medium-low, so you get a high simmer or low boil. Make a good mental note of the vinegar level in the pan; the goal is to reduce it by at least half. You will not be able to tell the achieved thickness until it cools completely. If it didn't get as thick as you wanted, bring back to the stove and cook longer. Move from the pot into a container while still warm, to reduce waste/loss.

Other Ingredients:

You may add Berries or a piece of fruit such as pear, peach, tangerine, orange peel or fig to the simmer, to infuse flavor.

Depending on the sensitivity of your spouse's sense of smell, consider opening the windows as you simmer, so to avoid an earful.

Use it sparingly on salads, tofu or veggies like Brussels sprouts, asparagus or cauliflower; not only is it expensive, but it also has a very intense flavor.

Some people even like it over Vanilla vegan ice cream.

Shortcut: to save time and get better yield, you may cheat by using about one tablespoon of sugar and one tablespoon of cornstarch to one cup of Balsamic vinegar. Add the cornstarch while the vinegar is still cold or dissolved in a bit of cold water whisking well, to avoid lumps. You'll then only need to reduce it by ¼, not by half.

Ginger Sesame

 10 minutes    1 Pint

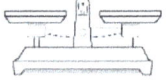
¼ cup tahini
1 large carrot
1 clove garlic
1-2 teaspoons ginger powder
1 teaspoon salt
1 tablespoon sugar
¼ teaspoon turmeric (optional)
¼ teaspoon paprika (optional)
2 Tablespoons lemon juice
2 Tablespoon Dijon mustard
~1 cup water

This is a deliciously rich and lean dressing; the thickness comes naturally from the carrot.

Use in salads, sandwiches, wraps and lukewarm bowls. You may try it, but I'm not a fan of this dressing served hot. Also works as a dip.

Ginger Sesame

Add all ingredients to the blender and blend without mercy, for several minutes, until very smooth.

Tip: for a smoother dressing, roast or boil the carrot before blending.

Brown Sauce (Gravy)

 40 minutes  1 Quart

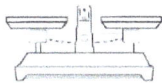

¼ cup whole wheat flour
1 onion
½ carrot
½ red pepper
1 rib celery
4 mushrooms
1 tomato
½ Tablespoon salt
1 cup red wine
3 cloves garlic
1 quart water
1 Tablespoon Braggs Aminos or tamari/soy sauce
1 Tablespoon paprika
3 sprigs of parsley, chopped
1 Tablespoon sugar, agave or maple syrup

This one takes some hands-on effort and is for special occasions, like a Thanksgiving plant-based loaf (page 127).

Heat a pot on medium-high. Cut the veggies in rough chunks if you will blend or strain it, or in neat dices if you will keep them in the sauce. Add the flour and onions to the pot and roast them stirring frequently. As the onions brown, add other veggies in stages, not to create too much moisture. The goal is to roast the veggies to dark brown with blackened edges, about 15 minutes, which will color the sauce and give depth to the flavor. Stir constantly. As the veggies dry and begin to stick to the pan, add the wine in small amounts. Let all the wine dry (au sec). Once you are done with the wine, add a bit of water anytime it gets completely dry.

Once the veggies are browned, add the quart of water and the seasoning, whisking it to mix well, until it comes to boil. Let it cook for a few minutes, and you should have a thick brown sauce or gravy. Strain for a clearer sauce or blend for a creamier thicker sauce. You may add a ¼ cup of raw cashews when you blend for an even smoother and creamier sauce.

Buffalo Sauce

 10 minutes  10 oz

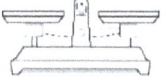
1 cup Mayo *(page 22)*
¼ cup hot sauce
½ teaspoon salt
1 teaspoon paprika
½ teaspoon garlic powder
1 teaspoon vinegar
1 teaspoon sugar

Buffalo Sauce

This one is quick and easy:

Mix all ingredients in a bowl or blender.

If you like it spicier, chop and add a few habaneros or jalapeno peppers.

Use in sandwiches, wraps, and salads or for dipping anything, like our Cauliflower Bites *(page 130)*

Curry Mayo

 10 minutes  10 oz

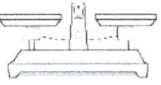
1 cup Mayo *(page 22)*
1 teaspoon hot sauce
½ teaspoon salt
1-2 teaspoons Curry Powder
½ teaspoon garlic powder
1 teaspoon Dijon Mustard

There was a place in my childhood days that served a very successful curry burger. I now love this dressing with my veggie burgers.

Curry Mayo

Mix all ingredients in a bowl with a whisk or in a blender.

Use in sandwiches, wraps, and salads or for dipping anything, like our Cauliflower Bites *(page 130)*.

Spicy Peanut

 10 minutes   1 ½ Pints

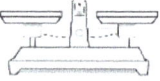
~¾ cup peanuts or peanut butter
1 pint water
2 Tablespoons lemon juice
2 cloves garlic
1 teaspoon salt
1 teaspoon ginger powder
1-2 teaspoons soy sauce
1-2 teaspoons hot sauce
1-2 teaspoons sugar

This one starts as American as peanut butter, gets an Asian touch and works beautifully with a Caribbean jerk hot sauce or jerk spice mix.

 Add all ingredients to the blender and blend well, until very smooth. Can be used for hot or cold dishes.

Other ingredient options:
- 2 roasted garlic cloves and ¼ roasted onion
- Jerk spice mix or Thai spice mix.
- Your preferred herb or spice: cilantro, parsley, basil, lemongrass.

Shiish! Too runny, or too salty: Blend in a bit more peanuts of peanut butter. If you are out of peanuts, you may use a piece of tofu, or a few raw cashews or tahini, or a bit of thickener, such as cornstarch. If you intend to heat it in a pot, the thickener will activate, and it will need more water and, perhaps, a bit more seasoning.

Nice touch: using a fresh chili instead of hot sauce will give it a fresh flavor.

Red Pepper Coulis

 10 minutes    1 Pint

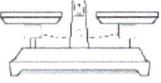
1 large red pepper
½ onion
2 garlic cloves
¼ cup cashew (optional)
1 ½ cups water, vegetable stock or plant milk
1 teaspoon salt

This is another versatile sauce that can be used with almost anything. It can be a dip for oven-fried potatoes, or it may be a salad or bowl dressing.

Red Pepper Coulis

 Roughly cut the pepper and onion, peel the garlic and roast them all on a pan or in the oven until you see a few burnt spots (adds to the color and brings depth to flavor).

Then move it to a blender with all other ingredients and blend until very smooth. Adjust the water, if necessary.

Other Ingredients

You may use yellow or green peppers. It will, of course, render a different color. It will also be less sweet so you may want to add a teaspoon of sugar.

Mushroom Gravy

 20 minutes  1 Quart

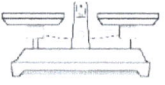
1 pound mushrooms (stems and all)
1 large onion
3 garlic cloves
2 Tablespoons - ¼ cup soy sauce
1 quart water
1-2 cups raw cashews
1 teaspoon salt
2 Tablespoons cornstarch

This gravy is very versatile, and I make it often at home. It can be a sauce for pasta or dress any vegan patty, lentil or bean loaf or even biscuits. It can be made into a soup with a bit more water or plant milk. You may thicken it into a nice spread, and, I must confess, I have been caught at home eating it from the fridge, with a spoon.

Mushroom Gravy

 Preheat a pot on high. Add small-diced onions and sliced or quartered mushrooms (using or adding Portobellos is a plus in flavor), reduce the heat to medium-high and roast them to a nice tan, adding a bit of water at times, as it starts to stick. You may definitely use the Portobello stems, just make sure to clean them thoroughly and roast them whole or in big chunks, so it will be easier to find and pick them all out for blending. Mince the garlic and add it toward the end to avoid the taste of burnt garlic.

Remove ½ of the veggies into a blender (the remainder will garnish the sauce) and blend well with the water, cashews and other ingredients. Return the blended sauce to the pan and bring it back to simmer. Cook longer to thicken; add water to thin.

Other Ingredients: To replace the cashews, you may use white beans, or a total 2-3 Tablespoons of cornstarch and replace all or part of the water with plant milk. Or you can use canned coconut milk with 1-2 Tablespoons of cornstarch, which will add a bit of coconut flavor (which I welcome).

If you are not a fan of mushrooms, replace them with red peppers, asparagus or butternut squash. Or you may add some of these ingredients to the mushrooms.

Tomato Sauce – From Scratch

 40 minutes to 2 hours   1 Pint

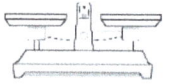
6-10 large tomatoes
1-2 large onions
5 cloves of garlic
1 carrot
1 teaspoon salt
½ teaspoon sugar
½ teaspoon basil, oregano or Italian seasoning

It takes a lot of tomatoes to make home-made tomato sauce from scratch, and it is nearly impossible to get the deep red color you get from store-bought. As an alternative, a topping of fresh diced tomatoes for you pasta works beautifully; in that case, skip the steps of blending and reducing the sauce, and consider adding a nice handful of thin-sliced spinach or kale, and a sprinkle of Nutritional yeast when plating.

Preheat a pot on the stove to high. Dice the tomatoes (peeling is optional) and onions in about ½" dice. Mince the garlic and shred the carrots. If you will blend the sauce, any rough cut is fine. Reduce the heat to medium-high Roast until nicely tanned, about or 5-10 min. Choose if you want a chunky sauce or if you prefer it blended, and then blend some or all the veggies.

If you blended, move it back to the pot, add the seasoning and bring to boil, then simmer. At this point, you can eat it at any time. From now on, the longer you cook, the sweeter and redder the sauce will be. Italian chefs recommend simmering from as little as 30 minutes to as long as 3 hours, lid on. Whenever too dry, add a bit more water. If you blended the sauce, the foamy look will also disappear as you cook longer.

Nice touch: any tomato sauce improves dramatically when you use fresh basil, oregano and/or parsley.

Tomato Sauce – Fixing the Store-Bought

 20 minutes   1 Pint

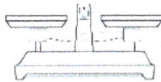

1 pint tomato sauce or 1 cup of tomato puree
1 large onion
5 cloves of garlic
1 carrot
2 mushrooms
½ to 1 teaspoon salt
1 teaspoon sugar
½ teaspoon basil, oregano or Italian seasoning

Companies that jar tomato, tomato sauce and pasta have advantages over us: they get their tomatoes cheaper and riper, and they also have better equipment to "sun-dry" and cook the tomatoes, so they get a very concentrated and red sauce. On the downside, the other chunky vegetables and seasonings that come in the sauce get soggy and lose flavor by sitting in the sauce for months.

My suggestion is that you focus on getting the nicely ripe and concentrated tomatoes in the jar, not worrying much about the veggies in it; those are easy to add. Get the basic stuff, only or mostly tomatoes, whole, diced, or pureed. There is no need to buy any fancy brand, just read the labels choosing one with fewer preservatives and no sugar, and watch for things that shouldn't be there, like milk protein.

Preheat a pot on the stove at high. Dice the onions and mushroom, mince the garlic and shred the carrots. Reduce the heat to medium-high and roast the veggies until nicely tanned, about 5-10 min. Decide whether you want a chunky sauce or if you prefer it blended, and then blend some or all the veggies. If you blended, pour it back to the pot, add the seasoning, and bring to simmer, add a bit of water if needed and it's ready. If you blended the sauce, the foamy look will also disappear as you cook a bit longer.

Other Ingredients: Peppers of any kind work well. Add Cashew Cream or blend some or all of the sauce with a ¼ cup of cashews for a creamy tomato sauce.

Nice touch: Any tomato sauce improves significantly when using fresh basil, oregano and/or parsley.

Creamy Tomato Sauce

 10 minutes    12-14 oz

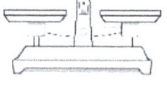 1 pint tomato sauce
¼ - ½ cup cashews
¼ cup water

or

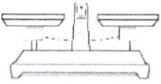 1 pint tomato sauce
2 Tablespoons to ¼ cup tahini

or

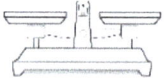 1 pint tomato sauce
½ - 1 cup canned coconut milk

Creamy tomato, using cashews

 Put all items in the blender, then heat in the pot, and it's ready to serve.

Mild Pesto

 15 minutes   1 Pint

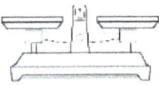
½ cup walnuts
½ cup cashews
3 cloves garlic
1 teaspoon salt
1 teaspoon lemon juice (helps keep it bright green)
1 teaspoon nutritional yeast
½ bunch basil
8 oz spinach
¼ cup water

Pesto is a delicious sauce or dip, but it's also a calorie bomb. Also, some people find the garlic and basil to be a bit overwhelming. This recipe eliminates the added oil and adds the goodness of spinach while preserving the great flavors.

Pesto is very versatile. Can be a sauce for pasta, a dressing for salads, sandwiches or a nice spread.

Pesto

Blend all ingredients but the water in a food processor, or blender (will require a tamper/pusher), until you reach a smooth paste; a few chunks are desirable. Do not add water until the very end, or it will make the pesto muddy and brown. Once it's nicely blended, add water and pulse a few times to mix.

Mild Curry

 10 minutes   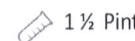 1 ½ Pint

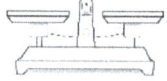
1 pint canned coconut milk
1 cup water
1-2 Tablespoons curry powder
1 Tablespoon cornstarch
1 teaspoon cumin
1 teaspoon coriander
1 teaspoon turmeric
1 teaspoon garlic powder
½ Tablespoon salt
½-1 Tablespoon sugar

There are thousands of ways of making curries; not only do they vary significantly within regions in India, but they are also considerably different in Thailand or in the Caribbean. Curries don't need to be very hot, spice-wise, so don't feel intimidated by it.

Potato, peas, pepper, carrot, onion, mushroom and eggplant, in Mild Curry sauce

If you are a curry lover, you may eventually want to make your own mix, adjusting ingredients to

taste. It's even better to mix whole seeds and grind fresh when cooking. Curries typically contain combinations of cumin, coriander, turmeric, paprika, mustard, cayenne, ginger, cinnamon, and nutmeg. It also includes flavors deemed very strong for us in the western hemisphere, like cardamom, anises, fennel seed, and celery seed, so I use those in moderation.

Add all ingredients to the blender and blend well, until very smooth. While best for hot dishes, I even have it cold, as a dip for raw cauliflower.

Other ingredient options:

You may use another plant milk, such as soy, almond, or cashew. Canned coconut milk is thicker than other carton plant milks; so you may need to adjust with a tablespoon or two of a thickener like cornstarch. You would need to bring it back to simmer for the thickener to activate.

- add your preferred hot sauce or chili powder to spice it up
- add 1 cup of tomato sauce or 1/2 cup tomato paste, and one teaspoon of ginger for a mild Tikka Masala style
- make a Thai variation adding a bit of, cilantro, basil, and lemongrass. Peanut butter works too.
- use Jerk seasoning for Caribbean fire.

Red Curry

Add to the Mild Curry recipe:
1-2 Tablespoons of paprika
2 medium red chilies, fresh or dried or ½ red bell pepper
½ bunch cilantro and/or 3-5 leaves of basil
1 Tablespoon lemon juice or 1 rib lemongrass
½ to 1 Tablespoon sugar

Cauliflower Cheese Sauce

 20 minutes    1 Quart

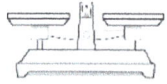
1 large onion
4 mushrooms
½ carrot
3 cloves garlic
½ of a cauliflower (or 2 large potatoes)
1 pint water
1 cup plant milk or ¼ cup of raw cashews
1 teaspoon turmeric
1 teaspoon Paprika
1 Tablespoon miso or mustard
2 Tablespoons tahini or peanut butter
1 Tablespoon nutritional yeast
½ Tablespoon salt

A very healthy version of a cheese sauce. It will not taste just like the whiz from the jar or the Mac 'n Cheese from the blue box; just a similar structure. This can also be done with potatoes, instead of cauliflower.

 Heat a pan on high. Add all the veggies, roughly cut, and roast them to a nice tan, adding a bit of water at times as it starts to stick. Add garlic toward the end to avoid tasting burnt garlic.

Remove all the veggies into a blender and blend well with the water and other ingredients. Return the blended sauce to the pan and bring it back to simmer. Cook longer to thicken or add water to thin.

Shiish! Too runny. Whisk in a tablespoon of cornstarch or take some of the sauce into the blender and blend raw cashews into the sauce.

Mac and Cheese

Cook one pack of whole-wheat macaroni, strain, and mix with the Cauliflower Cheese Sauce bin the pot. Serve, or bake in the oven, with or without breadcrumbs, for ~10-15 minutes at 350°, until a nice browning at the top. You may also use the Cashew Cheese recipe *(page 33)*, without the agar.

The Basics

Basic Bread

1 ½ hours (20 minutes hands-on)   2 small loaves

1½ cups of water
1 Tablespoon of yeast
2 teaspoons sugar

4 cups of whole-wheat flour
1-2 teaspoons salt
½ cup applesauce (optional; makes a softer bread)
½ cup oats or other grains (optional)

Easy recipe, which just requires a bit of patience because the dough must rise before baking.

Basic Bread

Add 1 ½ cups of lukewarm water, yeast, and sugar to a bowl, stir of whisk it and let it wake up and foam; about 15 minutes. If it doesn't foam, the yeast is dead, and the bread won't rise. Yeast is happiest in lukewarm water, but not too hot, for it will die in water over 120°. So we are looking for a temperature that feels comfortable and mildly warm to our skin, which is in the upper 90°s.

Add all other ingredients and mix well with a mixer or by hand. Adjust the flour and water for the dough consistency: if you are baking in a bread pan, you want a very thick batter, thick enough to barely release from the side of the bowl, but not firm enough to stand in a shape. If you are baking on a tray, you need firmer dough that will hold its shape. If you are not using a silicon surface in good condition, you may brush a little bit of oil on it.

If using bread-baking pans, fill each pan to about ½ with the dough. Or cut the dough in as many pieces you want for the tray. The volume will eventually double or triple.

Let the gluten relax, and the dough rise, about 45 minutes to one hour. This process is called proofing and works best at lukewarm temperatures, so look for a cozy spot in your kitchen, perhaps by the fridge or inside the microwave.

Preheat the oven to 325° for smaller loaves or 300 for larger loaves, and bake until you see a light to medium tan, about 18-20 for smaller loaves and 25-30 minutes for larger. Let it rest and set for a few minutes and enjoy.

Other Ingredients:

You can add all kinds of things to your bread, from peppers to olives to raisins. Play around!

Zucchini bread or banana bread: 1 shredded zucchini or 2 diced bananas, ½ cup sugar, 1 teaspoon cinnamon, and a pinch of nutmeg. Shredded pumpkin or squash also work.

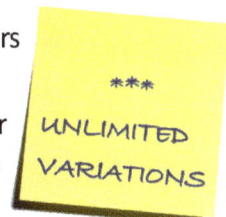

*** UNLIMITED VARIATIONS

Nut bread: 1 cup of chopped nuts. Adding the sugar and spices listed above for the Zucchini/Banana bread is optional.

For crustier bread, use higher gluten bread flour and bake at 350° for 15 to 20 minutes.

Basic Rice

 40 minutes (10 minutes hands-on)  4 servings

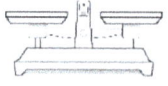
2 cups rice (I'm a big fan of the brown Basmati)
3 ¾ cups water
½ onion
½ carrot
1 celery rib
2 garlic cloves or 1 teaspoon garlic powder
1 teaspoon salt

Basic Rice cooked with carrot, onion, and garlic

 Finely dice or chop the veggies (which are optional) and roast in a pan until lightly brown, about 3 minutes, then add the rice, then the water, and bring to simmer. The cooking time will depend on the rice: white rice typically cooks in 20-25 minutes in low heat after it starts to simmer. Brown rice cooking time can vary greatly but averages 35-50 minutes. You can tell when it looks dry and you see those large holes across the top. Let the rice sit for a few minutes after cooked. A pot is perfectly fine, but a rice cooker or a slow cooker will make life easier.

Other ingredient options:

I like to add veggies when cooking rice because it flavors the rice and add nutrition, and replaces the need for buying vegetable stock. If you will eat the rice with beans, chili, or tasty casseroles, you may just cook the rice with seasoned water (salt, garlic powder, and other seasoning of your choice). You may replace the water and the veggies for the water equivalent in vegetable stock.

How to mess it up:

Don't mess with the rice while it's cooking; it will make it sticky. Don't stir and don't even look at it funny. Loosen (fluff) the rice with a fork only after it's cooked, and a bit cooled.

If you add too much water, it will overcook. You may try to drain the excess water, but you will inevitably have to let the rice absorb the excess water, with the heat on or off.

Nice touch:

Add ½ cup of quinoa and a cup of water for more sophisticated rice. All quinoas have similar nutritional properties; the red quinoa will be more noticeable.

Add a pinch of saffron for flavor and color, or a teaspoon of turmeric when the rice is cooking. The taste and color will be less noticeable in brown rice.

Other Grains that can be cooked with this same recipe:

Grain	Grain:Water[1]	Cooking Time[2]
Barley	1:3	50 min
Bulgur	1:2	15 min
Farro	1:2½	35 min
Millet	1:2½	30 min
Spelt Berries	1:3½	50 min
Quinoa	1:2	15 min
Brown Rice	1:2 (just short of 2)	40 min
Wheat Berries	1:3½	50 min

[1] *Cups of water per cup of grain; grain shown first, then water.*
[2] *Approximate cooking time in simmering water in a regular pot.*

Mashed Potatoes

 25 minutes    4 servings

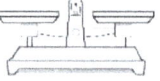 **3-5 large Russet, Yukon or Chef's potatoes**
1 cup Cashew Cream *(page 30)*, **or plant milk**
3 garlic cloves
1 teaspoon of salt
1 teaspoon nutritional yeast (optional)

Mashed Potatoes

It's hard not to love Mashed Potatoes, and it is really simple to make. I usually don't even peel the potatoes; I just rinse, scrub and rough-cut them, so I get all the nutrients and fiber from the skin.

The ideal potatoes for mashing are the types that are more starchy and less waxy, like the Chef's, Russet or Yukon Gold. Red or White potatoes are better for roasting or boiling and may turn the mashed potatoes into a waxy paste if you overmix it. If you are using these waxier potatoes, you may want to overcook them a bit and mash them very gently.

 Fill a pot halfway with cold or faucet lukewarm water (will boil faster). Rinse, scrub and cut the potatoes into rough cubes or slices, and place them straight in the water as you cut them. It is not necessary to peel the potatoes, but you may do so for a smoother texture.

Season water with salt and bring to boil. Simmer until potatoes are fully cooked, 15-20 minutes, depending on the potato.

Strain the potatoes. Don't rinse them, because they keep absorbing water if you do, and you because want to mash them while still hot.

Add the potatoes, garlic, and seasoning to a bowl, then mash it using use a mixer with the paddle attachment, a ricer or a masher, or mash by hand with a large fork. I like a few little chunks of potato here and there for a more rustic feel.

Moist absorption will vary with the potatoes; you may add more cashew cream, plant milk, or water as needed. It will dry a bit more after you stop mashing.

It will work well with Mushroom Gravy *(page 44)*, or many of the sauces like the Red Pepper Coulis *(page 43)*, Spicy Peanut *(page 42)* and Zesty Tahini *(page 21)*, Mild curry sauce *(page 50)*, or just tomato sauce. I even like it with Mayo *(page 22)*.

Hint: make a double batch and have some leftovers for a Shepherd's pie *(page 86)*.

Black Beans

 3 hours (20 minutes hands on)   4 servings

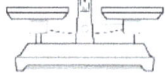
1 pound black beans (dry)
1 Tablespoon of garlic powder
1 Tablespoon cumin
½ Tablespoon coriander
1 Tablespoon salt
1 Tablespoon sugar
3 garlic cloves
1 Tablespoon Tamari or Soy Sauce
1 onion
1 tomato
1 carrot
2 ribs of celery
5 sprigs cilantro

Black Beans

My native country, Brazil, and many other regions in Latin America and Central America have the combination of rice and beans as the foundation of their nutrition; and for good reason: it is a source of complete protein, i.e., it contains all essential amino acids, and it's also an excellent source of complex carbs, minerals, and micronutrients. Add to it a variety of veggies, and you have a meal as nutritionally complete, as it gets, and for less than $2 per serving. Who said eating healthy is expensive?

I'm aware that some people worry that beans will cause them flatulence. It can happen for people not used at all to eating legumes. The risk can be reduced by soaking the beans for at least 8 hours and discarding the soaking water, and by cooking beans longer, until they are very tender. Because Brazilians eat beans with rice, not as a soup, we like it as a very thick stew, which requires long cooking, up to as much as 4 hours of simmering.

Soak beans overnight, or for at least one hour in water seasoned with a tablespoon of garlic powder. Drain, rinse and add the beans to a pot. Add water until it covers the beans by one inch. Bring to boil, reduce temperature to low and simmer for 1.5 to 4 hours, lid on, occasionally stirring so the bottom doesn't burn. It is better, to preserve flavor, to roast separately and add all the other veggies diced, and the seasoning at the end, yet, you may find it more practical to add all ingredients to the pot at the beginning and let it all cook together. Let it cook.

Seriously, put the timer on and go do something else, don't drive yourself crazy staring at the pot. The longer it cooks, the thicker and richer it will be (and it will be even better the next day, when you reheat the leftovers). Take a peek every half hour, give it a gentle stir, and see if it needs more water. Chop the cilantro and add it right before serving.

Slow cooker: if you have a slow cooker, add all ingredients but the cilantro to the pot and use the designed program or manual slow-cook for 6-8 hours. If the beans don't get as thick as you like, reduce the water for the next time.

Shortcut: 2 pounds of canned beans, drained and rinsed. Instead of cooking long, blend ~1/3 of the beans in 1 quart of water, roast the veggies and mix it all in a pot. Bring to simmer. It will not have the same taste, texture, and color, but it's a shortcut.

You may serve it by itself, as a soup, or over rice, over quinoa or grains, with tofu, seitan, and tempeh. You may blend the whole soup if you prefer. It will look greyish right after you blend, but it will recompose into a nice texture and color if you bring it back to the pot and simmer for a while.

Shiish: Too runny. Blend one or two ladles of the beans and return to the pot, bringing it to boil.

Lentils

 45 minutes (20 minutes hands on) 4 servings

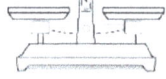
2 cups dried lentils (any color)
~6 cups water
1 teaspoon garlic powder
1 teaspoon cumin
1 teaspoon coriander
1 teaspoon sugar
1 teaspoon paprika
1/8 teaspoon cinnamon
2 teaspoon salt
½ cup tomato sauce (optional)
1 teaspoon soy sauce or tamari
2 cloves garlic
½ onion
1 pepper
1 tomato
1 potato
1 carrot
2 ribs of celery

Red Lentils

Lentils are to the Middle East and South Asia what beans are for Central and South America. They are used for stews and soups and also serve as a base for sauces, like curries of many varieties. Lentils are found in a diversity of colors and sizes, and they cook much faster than beans. The challenge with lentils is to cook them just right, for they overcook easily and get mushy. Like most grains and legumes, different lentils absorb water a bit differently and cook in different times. Thus, getting the water level perfectly right is relevant, and you need to taste the doneness about every minute after 15 minutes of simmering. When you cook your preferred type of lentil, take notes as to the amount of water and cooking time.

Lentils will cook a bit faster if you soak them for one hour, but it can be done without soaking.

Add the lentils to a large pot with all the seasoning and the minced garlic. Either add all the other veggies diced, or roast them separately and add them at the end. Add water until it covers the lentils by ½ inch, about 6 cups. Bring to boil, reduce temperature and simmer for ~17-20 minutes. Like the beans, the longer it cooks, the thicker and creamier it will be; however, unlike the beans, the lentils will fall apart when overcooked. After some 40 minutes, the lentils will pretty much dissolve, so keep an eye on it if you like the lentils with a firmer texture.

Slow cooker: if you have a slow cooker, lookup if it has specific instructions for lentils, for the bean program will likely overcook the lentils.

You may serve it by itself, as a soup, or over rice, quinoa or grains, with tofu, seitan, and tempeh. You are very welcome to blend the soup if you prefer a cream of lentils.

Hint: Make a larger batch; use leftovers for the Shepherd's Pie *(page 86)*.

Shiish: I overcooked the darn thing! It probably still tastes alright, so, if you just dislike the texture, blend it into a creamy soup.

Too runny! Blend one or two ladles of the lentils and return to the pot, bringing it to a boil. If you used way too much water, there is a good chance it will become overcooked before you get it thick, which brings us back to the decision of whether you want to blend it all.

Tofu

 25 minutes  4 -8 servings

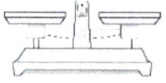
1 or 2 packs extra firm tofu
¼ cup soy sauce or tamari
~2 cups water
1 Tablespoon lemon pepper (optional)
1 teaspoon lemon juice (optional)

Tofu, marinated with soy sauce and lemon pepper, then baked

I have heard people say they hate tofu. I have also seen many change their mind when tofu is cooked with a bit of love. Tofu doesn't taste like anything out of the pack, but it can taste truly delicious when you marinate and bake.

Marinating is a must. Baking is recommended. Sautéing and grilling are a bit more challenging because it's harder to remove the moisture and give the tofu a nice consistency.

If you just pull it out of the pack onto the pan and quickly brown the outside of it, it still has way too much moisture inside, and it won't absorb much flavor. It needs to marinate and cook slowly. If you can't bake it, put the burner on mid-low and have patience.

Marinate the tofu for at least one hour in watered down soy sauce (pure soy sauce will make it too salty), about ¼ cup of soy sauce for 2 cups of water.

If the tofu is firm enough, cut it into cubes or slices before marinating. If it is a bit soft or flaky, marinate it whole and cut it right before baking it.

I like to add a bit of lemon pepper; feel free to add your favoring seasoning, like Old Bay, Jamaican jerk, Mexican mix, etc.

If you are in a hurry, pull the tofu out of the pack, drain it with a strainer, cut in cubes or slices and put it in a bowl. Pour about 2 tablespoons of soy sauce into the bowl with any additional seasoning you like, like lemon pepper or Easy Veggies Seasoning *(page 19)* and toss it gently and thoroughly to season it evenly. This will season the tofu, but it will not penetrate as deep as the marinade.

 Preheat the oven to 325-350°. Spread the tofu over a tray and roast for about 15 minutes, until nicely browned.

You may use a preheated pan in mid-low temperature on the stove and roast each side for about 5-10 minutes, but the oven will be more effective to dehydrate the tofu to a nice and firm consistency.

Meals

Fried Rice

 20 minutes   2-4 servings

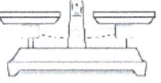
1 onion
½ pepper
4 mushrooms
1 carrot
½ block of tofu (of any kind)
¼ cup of soy sauce or tamari
2 Tablespoons of sesame seeds or tahini
1 teaspoon of turmeric (optional, if you'd like the tofu to look eggier)
Salt to taste, if you feel you need it
3 cups of cooked rice (page 55)

Fried Rice with onion, peppers, zucchini, tomato, mushroom, spinach, tofu, and sesame seeds

Great for cleaning up leftovers from your fridge; if you dice it up, pretty much anything goes.

Preheat a pan on medium-high. Dice the onions and pepper, slice or quarter the mushrooms, shred or dice the carrot and crumble the tofu, directly to the pan. Roast the veggies and tofu until they start to brown, then add the seasoning and roast a bit more. Use a bit of water if it starts to stick to the pan.

Add the rice and soy sauce and mix well with a spatula.

Other Ingredients: Whatever you have, fresh, frozen, canned, you really can't mess this up: broccoli, kale, spinach, cauliflower, potatoes, sweet potatoes, squash, corn, chickpeas, beans, peas, string beans, etc. Just dice it up or slice it thin.

Other ingredients: add your favorite seasoning or spice mix, like Thai seasoning, Mexican seasoning, curry, or Sriracha.

Nice Touch: serve with a good drizzle of one of our sauces, like the Spicy Peanut *(page 42)*, **Mild Curry** *(page 50)*, **Zesty Tahini** *(page 21)* or **Mushroom Gravy** *(page 44)*.

Sushi Rice

 50 minutes (10 minutes hands on)   5 cups

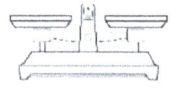

2 cups short grain brown rice (like sushi rice or Arborio)
3 ¾ cups water
1/3 cup rice vinegar
1 Tablespoon salt
1 Tablespoon soy sauce
2 Tablespoons of raw sugar

Add only the rice and water to the pot. The cooking time will depend on the rice: White rice typically cooks in 20 minutes in low heat after simmer. Brown rice may take from 35 minutes to as much as one hour. Let the rice sit for a few minutes after cooked. A pot is perfectly fine, but a rice cooker or slow cooker will make life easier. It's ready when all the water dried.

After the rice is cooked, move the rice to a non-metallic bowl, mix the seasoning, and spread the rice flat against the walls of the bowl and let it cool. Serious sushi makers use a large and flat wooden bowl called *hangiri*, which helps absorb heat and excessive moisture. A plastic or glass bowl will be ok for home use. Metal bowls don't get along with the vinegar.

Other ingredient options:

In America, we tend to like sweeter and saltier sushi rice. Adjust the seasoning to your taste and keep notes. You will taste less of the seasoning on the brown rice than you will on white rice. Some people add Sake, but I wouldn't waste a fine bottle of sake on it. I like to add sesame seeds to my sushi rice. You may use other types of vinegar if you can't find rice vinegar, but reduce the amount by half, to avoid adding too much of a foreign flavor.

Nice touch:

Add ½ cup of quinoa and a cup of water for more sophisticated rice. All quinoas have similar nutritional properties; the red quinoa will be more noticeable.

Sushi Rolls

 35 minutes   10 rolls

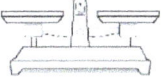
1 recipe of sushi rice *(page 68)*
10 sheets nori sushi seaweed
1 medium carrot
1 cucumber
1 large avocado
10 asparagus spears or a small jar of roasted or pickled red peppers
Jar of roasted sesame seeds
Sushi mat

Don't be intimidated; it's simpler and easier than it seems. Even if it doesn't look like the Michelangelo of sushis the first time, it will be perfectly fine.

Slice off the skin of the cucumber, 1/8" deep, then cut it into very thin strips. Set the remaining inner part of the cucumber aside, and munch on it as you finish the sushi.

Peel the carrot, cut it in 1/8" slices, then into very thin strips.

Cut the avocado in half, lengthwise. Remove the seed, cut each half in strips, lengthwise, before scooping the avocado out of the skin with a large spoon.

Measure the asparagus against the width of the nori, cut off the bottom of the asparagus and save it for the next time you will roast veggies or make soup.

Place the nori on the sushi mat, lengthwise. Cover 1/2 of the nori (the side closest to you) with a 1/4" layer of rice. Wet the tip of your fingers in water to help spreading the rice without sticking to your fingers. Sprinkle sesame seeds over the rice. Align a full assortment of the cut veggies in the center of the rice, perpendicular to the shape of the nori.

Sushi roll with brown rice, avocado, roasted pepper, cucumber and carrot

Starting with the closest edge of the nori with the rice on it, lift the edge of the nori and roll it over to touch the edge of the rice layer in the center of the nori. Continue to roll over the nori that is not covered in rice, as tight as you can with your hands.

Now, use the mat to make it tighter, rolling in over the sushi roll, firmly, but not squashing it in anger. If the rice is still lukewarm, there is probably enough moisture to set the nori around. If the rice is cold, use your fingertips to moist the edge of the nori not covered with rice, before you roll it.

Let it set for a couple of minutes before cutting the roll into about eight ~3/4" pieces. Serve with soy sauce.

Other ingredient options:

There are lots of fruits and vegetables you can try in your sushi roll: radishes, turnip, parsnip, sweet potato (cooked), tofu, beet and pickles of all variety. Mango, apple, kiwi, pear, pineapple, melon, etc.

Nice touch:

Green onions and chives make a nice garnish, inside or on top of the cut rolls. Sprinkled sesame seeds make a nice garnish too.

You may use a nice drop of any of the Mayo Variances *(Page 22 - 27)* on top of each slice of the cut rolls, for extra flavor and color. Or you may want to mix a tablespoon of Sriracha with a 1/2 cup of Mayo to make your own Sriracha Mayo.

To make your wasabi, get a small jar of Wasabi powder at the international aisle of your supermarket, scoop a tablespoon into a small container, and pour slow drizzles of water as you stir it into a creamy, but firm paste. You may also mix it with mayo, for a wasabi mayo.

How to mess it up:

In Japanese tradition, it would take 5 years of apprenticeship for a cook to be trusted to make sushi rice independently. Yours will have its flaws: perhaps too moist or too dry, or the seasoning is off. Taste it, fix if you can, and take notes for next time.

You may find it challenging to make the rolls tight, and the insides may crumble when you dip them in the soy sauce. You'll get the touch. Your 10th roll will look better than the 1st.

Chickpeas and Spinach

 20 minutes   2 servings

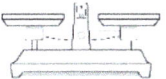
½ onion
3-5 garlic cloves
1 can of chickpeas
1 bag of spinach (or a bunch of kale)
¼ teaspoon cumin
½ teaspoon salt
1 teaspoon soy sauce or tamari
¼ cup cashew cream (optional)

Sometimes, it's just the simplest things that work so well! I used to love this recipe with lots of olive oil. I now love it without the oil.

Preheat a pan in mid-high, dice the onions and mince the garlic, then roast until lightly tanned. Don't burn the garlic. Add the chickpeas, let them roast for a bit, and then add the seasoning. While the veggies roast, pile up the spinach or kale and cut it in thin slices, in what the French call "chiffonade"; add it to the pot towards the end and let it soften. Serve and enjoy.

Tip: if using kale, push the kale leaves through the food processor, stems first, with the top slicing blade on. If you slice it super-thin, you don't need to remove the stems for cooked kale. You can do it with a knife too: pack and roll up the leaves and slice as thin as you can.

Chickpeas and Spinach, with a sprinkle of lemon pepper

Risotto - old fashioned way

 40 minutes   2 -4 servings

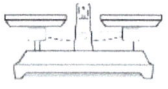
- 2 cups short-grain brown rice
- ~5 cups water (depends on evaporation)
- 1 onion
- ½ carrot
- ~10 mushrooms
- 1 celery rib
- 2 garlic cloves or 1 teaspoon garlic powder
- 1 teaspoon salt
- 1 teaspoon nutritional yeast (optional)

Risotto is traditionally made by slowly adding liquid to the cooking rice and stirring it constantly. Its creaminess comes from the released rice starch. This is a basic recipe, to which you may add about 12 ounces of any of your favorite vegetables, like butternut squash, pumpkin, mushroom, asparagus, peas, leeks, corn, etc.

Butternut Squash Risotto – old fashioned way

 Add the veggies to a medium skillet and sauté the vegetables until lightly browned. Keep it at medium heat, add the rice and then add 1 cup of water, and continue to add water when it dries, ½ cup at a time, stirring frequently. White rice will cook in about 20 minutes; brown rice may take twice as long. Taste the rice for doneness when it feels soft and creamy. Add more water if necessary.

Other ingredient options:

You may use other veggies in addition to or replacing the mushrooms, such as butternut squash, asparagus, red pepper, lemongrass, corn, peas, artichokes, chestnuts or sun-dried tomato.

Play around with seasonings, herbs, spices, and tamari. You may flavor risotto in a million ways. You may use veggie stock instead of water for extra flavor.

Replacing 1 cup of water with white wine is traditional. Red wine will make a pink risotto. I'll commit a WFPB heresy here and suggest a few drops of high-quality truffled oil.

Nice touch:

You may garnish your risotto by roasting a bit of your main vegetable separately and adding it to the plate. Fresh scallions are a versatile garnish.

Risotto - how everybody does it

 25 minutes  2-4 servings

2 cups short grain rice (like sushi rice or Arborio)
3 ¾ cups water
1 onion
½ carrot
~10 mushrooms
1 celery rib
2 garlic cloves or 1 teaspoon garlic powder
1 teaspoon salt
1 cup cashew cream *(page 30)*
1 teaspoon nutritional yeast (optional)

Stirring the risotto and slowly adding liquid takes hands-on attention, so, most people use cream and cheese to make it creamy. In our case, we will use cashew cream.

Mushroom Risotto, how everybody does it, from Basic Rice leftovers with white and Porcini mushrooms.

 If you have leftover cooked rice, skip the first 2 ingredients and start with roasting the veggies, then add 4 cups of cooked rice. If cooking rice from scratch, add the vegetables, rice, seasoning, and water to a medium pan, and cook the rice, as in the basic rice directions. White rice will cook in about 20 minutes; brown rice may take twice as long. Once the rice is cooked, add the cashew cream, and stir until hot.

Other ingredient options:

This is a basic recipe; you may add or replace other veggies for the mushrooms, such as butternut squash, asparagus, red pepper, lemongrass, corn, leeks, pumpkin, green peas, artichokes, beets, chestnuts, and sun-dried tomato.

Play around with seasonings, herbs, spices, and tamaris. You may flavor risotto in a million ways. I'll commit a WFPB heresy here and suggest a few drops of high-quality truffle oil. You may use veggie stock instead of water for extra flavor.

Replacing 1 cup of water with white wine is traditional. Red wine will make a pink risotto.

Nice touch: You may garnish your risotto by roasting a bit of your main vegetable separately, and adding it to the plate. Chopped fresh green onions are a versatile garnish.

Hint: Double the recipe and use the leftovers for Risotto Cakes of for stuffing peppers or cabbage leaves.

Risotto Cakes

If you like your risotto a bit crispier, or if you have risotto leftovers and would like to do something different with it, this is a great alternative.

Preheat the oven to 350° or a pan on mid-high. Once your risotto is chilled, it will be very firm; scoop a large spoonful of risotto and form into a ball in your hands, a bit larger than a golf ball. Place it on a baking sheet or pan and flatten it to a disk, about ½ to 1 inch tall. Bake for 10-15 minutes in the oven until nicely tanned or on the pan for 3-5 minutes on each side.

Tossing the cakes in whole-wheat breadcrumbs before roasting is a nice touch.

Couscous - a great friend of a quick meal

 25 minutes 4 servings

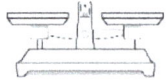
2 ½ cups water
1 teaspoon salt
Pinch of cinnamon powder
Pinch of ground nutmeg
½ teaspoon curry powder
2 cups whole wheat Moroccan couscous
½ onion
½ carrot
2 garlic cloves or 1 teaspoon garlic powder
1-2 pounds of random vegetables of your choice

Couscous with carrot, chickpea, peppers, corn, pea, onions, baked tofu, and Zesty Peanut sauce

Couscous is a perfect use for your leftover vegetables, and the beauty is that it cooks (or rehydrates) super-fast. Anything goes, fresh, frozen, canned, you really can't mess this up: broccoli, mushroom, peppers, kale, spinach, cauliflower, potatoes, sweet potatoes, squash, corn, chickpeas, beans, peas, string beans, etc.

In a medium pot, bring water with all the seasonings to a boil. Turn off the heat, add the couscous with a light stir, put the lid on, and let it sit while you roast the veggies in a skillet until lightly brown. Fluff the couscous with a fork, and then toss in the vegetables.

Nice touch:

You may garnish your couscous with fresh parsley and scallions. For extra flavor, use one of the sauces in this book, like the Zesty Tahini *(page 21),* Mild Curry *(page 50)* or Spicy Peanut *(page 42).*

Goes well with baked tofu, seitan or Soy Curls ™.

Last Minute Bowl

 15 minutes  2-4 servings

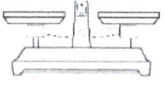
1 can of chickpeas or beans of any kind
1 can of corn
1 tomato
¼ onion
½ pepper
Handful of spinach
½ cup frozen peas
1 cup oats
½ cup Mayo *(page 22)* or any sauce from this book.
2 Tablespoons Dijon mustard
2 Tablespoons soy sauce

Last Minute Bowl with the recipe's sauce

Canned veggies are a lifesaver for a super-quick meal or for when there's nothing in the fridge. It is a good idea to mix in whatever fresh veggies you might have to bring up freshness to the bowl, even if all you have is an onion or a tomato.

Open the cans, drain and rinse the veggies. Dice the onion, tomato, pepper and whatever other vegetable you may have, and toss with the oats, seasoning, and sauce. For my wife, even just ketchup and mustard suffice. If you are using curry sauce or tomato sauce, you may like the taste better if you heat the veggies bowl.

***
UNLIMITED VARIATIONS

I personally don't mind the uncooked oats being a bit chewy. They bring the starchy component and good natural oils to the bowl. If you heat the bowl or let it sit for a few minutes, the oats will get softer.

Nice Touch: Serve over salad greens, spinach or massaged kale.

 You really can't go wrong with adding avocado or guacamole to a bowl.

Tacos

⏱ 15 minutes 📏 2 servings

½ onion
1 pepper
8 oz seitan, Soy Curls™ or tofu (optional)
2 oz spinach or kale
4 oz corn
6 tortillas
Cilantro dressing *(page 26)*

Tacos with avocado, sweet potatoes, kale, corn, Salsa and Cilantro Dressing

Tacos are another excellent opportunity for your leftover vegetables. Anything goes, fresh, frozen, canned, you really can't mess this up: tomato, mushroom, peppers, kale, sweet potatoes, squash, corn, beans, peas, string beans, etc.

There are several options of tortillas, the corn ones are gluten-free and are more susceptible to cracking, especially when they are not very fresh. The flour tortillas are more pliable, even in whole wheat.
My favorite is a type called soft corn, which includes a mix of corn flour with a bit of wheat.

Roast the onion, pepper, corn, and kale, and any other veggie you may have. I like sweet potatoes in the tacos too.

Warm up the tacos on a hot pan, oven or even microwave for a few seconds, just to make them pliable, and load them up.

If you prefer a hard shell, use a couple of heat resistant ramekins to hold a few folded tortillas in shape, like we do with bookends, and bake at 325° for about 10 minutes.

Nice Touch:

Make a recipe of Salsa and or Guacamole *(page 137)* and save the leftovers to munch with chips. The Cilantro Dressing *(page 26)* is a great match.

Veggie Curry

 40 minutes   4 servings

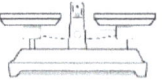
1 onion
1-2 peppers
6-8 mushrooms
1 cauliflower head
2 potatoes
2 carrots
2 ribs of celery
1 recipe of Mild curry sauce *(page 50)*

Veggie Curry with Red Curry and Rice and Quinoa

 Preheat the oven to 325° or a pot on mid-high. Roast diced potatoes, onions, peppers, carrot, sliced mushrooms, and celery for about 15 minutes. Meanwhile, break the cauliflower head into bite-size pieces, and mix the curry recipe in the blender. Add the curry sauce and the veggies to a large pot, and bring to boil. Check if the cauliflower and potatoes are fully cooked and simmer until they are. Add water or plant milk if it starts to dry or thicken too much.

Serve with rice, pasta, couscous, barley, faro, bulgur, quinoa or, my favorite: polenta.

Other Ingredients:

You may replace or add a variety of veggies to it: eggplant, edamame, squash, pumpkin, peas, broccoli, etc. You may pretty much make it all from your emergency stock of frozen and canned veggies and coconut milk.

Baked tofu, seitan, and tempeh are nice additions.

Cilantro and green onions are good garnish ideas.

Add one cup of tomato sauce or ½ cup of tomato paste to go in the Tikka Masala direction, or 2-4 Tablespoons of peanut butter and 2 sprigs of cilantro to go in the Massaman direction.

Mushroom Stroganoff

 30 minutes   2-4 servings

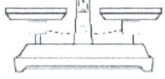
~10 mushrooms (stems and all)
2 Portobello mushrooms
2 cups peas or edamame
1 carrot
2 large onions
3 garlic cloves
1/4 cup soy sauce
1 quart water
1 cup raw cashews
1 teaspoon salt
1 Tablespoon cornstarch
1 teaspoon paprika
1 teaspoon dill

Mushroom Stroganoff over whole-wheat fusilli

Preheat a pot on high. Roast diced onions, thinly sliced mushrooms, and Portobellos. Roast the Portobellos' stems whole, so it's easy to pick them out for blending.

Blend ½ cup of the onions and mushrooms with the cashews, water, and seasoning and return to the pot. Add carrot and edamame and bring to boil and let simmer until the sliced carrots are cooked. Add water if necessary.

Serve over pasta (I like whole wheat fusilli), or over rice, couscous, polenta, barley, bulgur or quinoa.

Other ingredients:

You can use an extra ½ cup of cashews and skip the cornstarch.

You can use 1 can of coconut milk and one pint of plant milk instead of the water and cashews. Or you can use one quart of plant milk and 2 tablespoons of cornstarch.

Mushroom lovers want the mushrooms to shine. You may add more or more diverse mushrooms.

To make it more nutritionally interesting, add a variety of other veggies, as you please.

Nice Touch: Use fresh dill for the recipe and garnish. Note that dill has a very strong flavor. Add it slowly and taste it, until you find the right spot on your palate.

Shepherd's Pie

 35 minutes   4-6 servings

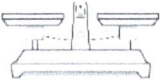
1 recipe of Mashed potatoes *(page 58)*.
1 large onion
2 ribs of celery
1 cup green peas
1 cup corn
1 carrot or sweet potato
1 pepper
2 cloves garlic
5 mushrooms
2 teaspoons salt or Easy Veggie Seasoning *(page 19)*
1 cup of cooked lentils, beans or chickpeas
2 cups tomato sauce or mushroom gravy *(page 44)*
1 Tablespoon soy sauce
1 Tablespoon cornstarch

Shepherd's Pie using Mushroom Gravy

A comfort food staple. It can be made with a variety of veggies and sauces. This is simple to make and always a family-pleasing recipe.

Preheat the oven to 350℉ or a pan on medium-high. Cut veggies in small dice and roast in the oven, or sauté in the pan until nicely browned. No need to roast the peas or corn. Mix all veggies (except for the mashed potatoes), seasoning and sauce, in a large bowl.

Spread the filling on the bottom of a baking dish or pan, or in single serving size oven-safe mold or bowl. Cover with the mashed potato and bake until the potatoes start to brown, about 15-20 minutes.

Shepherd's Pie filling

Other ingredients: Shredded seitan, baked tofu, texturized vegetable protein or tempeh work well.

Lentils make an excellent filling for Shepherd's pie. If you have leftover lentils, just add a few more veggies to it, and it's ready.

If you prefer the filling to be firmer under the mashed potatoes, as we did for Shepherd's pie in the picture, so it would stand, add another tablespoon of cornstarch to the sauce you are using, or as you mix with the veggies.

Nice touch: Make waves with a fork or spoon on top of the mashed potatoes. It will look nice when it browns. A touch of fresh herbs like parsley, rosemary, and thyme in the filling and a sprinkle for garnishing are also a nice touch.

Hint: If you made an extra batch of mash potatoes for a future Shepherd's Pie, you may store it spread flat on a tray, in the fridge, in about the same shape and size you need for the pie. When it is cold, you will be able to transpose it to the top of the shepherd's pie, without having to spread it over and disturb the filling.

Pasta Primavera

 25 minutes  4 servings

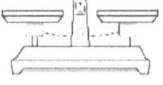
16oz whole wheat pasta
1 onion
4 cloves garlic
1 pepper
5 mushrooms
1 tomato
handful of spinach
1 cup peas
1 pint tomato sauce
1 teaspoon of salt

Pasta Primavera with Creamy Tomato Sauce

This is a basic pasta recipe, with infinite variations. You may use any style of pasta you prefer; I prefer fusilli because I believe it grabs the sauce a bit better. There are also many excellent gluten-free pasta choices available these days: brown rice, garbanzo, lentils, and various grains and legume flours.

Every pasta will cook a bit differently; follow the instructions on the pack, for timing. Take it off the stove a minute or two early, if you will reheat and cook it in the sauce for a bit.

Start with bringing water to boil in a large pot. Salt the water, with about one teaspoon of salt. Add your favorite shape of whole-wheat pasta to the boiling water and bring the heat down to low when the boiling stabilizes. Most whole-wheat pasta will cook in 12 minutes. Drain the pasta into a large strainer and bring the pot back to the stove for the veggies.

Chop all veggies and add them to the pot at mid-high heat, starting with the onion and ending with the tomato and spinach, once the other veggies are lightly browned. Add the tomato sauce and the strained past and mix well. Adjust the seasoning.

Nice touch: You may garnish with roughly chopped fresh basil and sprinkle nutritional yeast, for a "cheesy" taste.

Other Ingredients: Add your favorite veggies: broccoli, cauliflower, asparagus, sweet potato, kale, etc.

Add 1 cup of Cashew Cream *(page 30)* or Savory cashew cream *(page 32)* for a creamy tomato sauce. Replace the tomato sauce entirely for 1 pint of Savory cashew cream *(page 32)* for an Alfredo-style creamy sauce.

Polenta

 60 minutes (30 minutes hands-on)   4 servings

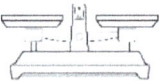
1 cup of polenta (yellow cornmeal)
½ cup quinoa (optional)
1 quart + 1 cup of water
1-2 teaspoons salt
1 teaspoon garlic powder

A favorite since I was a kid! Also very easy to make; and very versatile. Polenta and grits are essentially the same thing but made from different types of corn, with slightly different processes. Typically, polenta is made from a yellower corn and ground coarsely, and grits are made from whiter corn and ground finely. If all you have is grits, you may use it for polenta, even if the purists scream and shout.

Polenta with Mild Curry Sauce and green peas, roasted mushrooms, peppers, and onions

Add all ingredients to a large pot, bring to boil. Reduce the heat to mid-low and simmer for ~20-25 minutes stirring frequently (or the bottom will burn), until it forms a pasty consistency and you see bubbles, like lava. In fact, be careful with the bubbles; some will pop from the pot and may burn you like lava. Add more water if it is too dry before you reach 20 minutes.

At this point, it's perfectly edible, and you can scoop to a plate and serve. The next step is for aesthetics: use a high heat spatula to spread the polenta over a baking sheet, tray or Pyrex while still hot, and let it chill entirely. If your baking sheet is very scratched and has seen better days, you may need a parchment/wax paper or even brush it with a small amount of oil, so it doesn't stick.

Once chilled, run a thin pastry spatula or knife around the edges of the polenta to release. Place a cutting board over the tray (hovering over the polenta), and flip the tray over the cutting board. The chilled polenta will pop off the tray with a few taps on the middle of the tray.

Choose the shape you want to cut the polenta: cubes, squares, triangles (cutting the squares in ½, diagonally) or even in special shapes, with a cookie cutter (which will leave you a lot of trimmings to munch on). Reheat it in the oven or in a pot, with the sauce.

Traditional topping is a tomato sauce, to which you can add veggies.

Since polenta has plenty of starch, I'd choose less starchy veggies and leaves. It will work well with Mushroom Gravy *(page 44)*, or many of the sauces like Spicy Peanut *(page 42)* and Zesty Tahini *(page 21)*. I've come to like it a lot with Mild Curry Sauce *(page 50)*, which will terrify any Italian looking at this recipe.

***
UNLIMITED VARIATIONS

Polenta "Fries"

Tip: set some trimmings or slices of polenta aside, cut to the size of French fries or potato wedges. Roast them in the oven at 375-400, for about 10 minutes, until golden and crisp, but not burnt. It's a delicious snack or side.

Polenta Fries sprinkled with Easy Veggies Seasoning (page 19)

Enchiladas

 40 minutes — 10 enchiladas

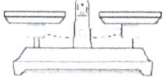

10 Tortillas (corn or wheat)
1 pound sweet potatoes (or regular potatoes)
1 onion
½ pepper
1 rib celery
3 cloves garlic
½ cup canned beans (any bean)
½ cup frozen or canned corn
1 cup chopped kale or spinach
1 teaspoon salt
hot sauce (as much as you like)
1 pint tomato sauce
5 sprigs cilantro
1 cup Savory cashew cream *(page 32)*

Enchiladas

 Preheat the oven to 325°. Dice the onions, pepper, celery, sweet potatoes, and garlic and roast at 325° for ~15 minutes.

Move all veggies to the bowl, along with the spinach, corn, and beans, and add ¼ cup of tomato sauce, salt, hot sauce and about ½ of the cilantro (chopped) and mix well. If you have a preferred seasoning mix, like lemon pepper, Old Bay or Mexican Seasoning, you may add it too. You may lightly mash the sweet potatoes to improve the binding.

Warm the tortillas to, at least, room temperature. Corn tortillas can be tricky to roll and may break or crack, especially those that sat on a supermarket shelf for long. Best you can do with those is to moisten them with a spray and warm them up. Wheat tortillas will be easier to roll. Pour one or two very generous spoonfuls of filling over the tortilla, roll them up and place them in a baking pan with the seam down.

Cover the enchiladas with tomato sauce, garnish with the cashew cream and bake for about 15-20 minutes at 350°.

Garnish with the chopped cilantro and serve.

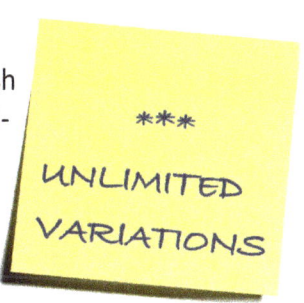

Other ingredient options:

Like many dishes in this book, the enchiladas give you an opportunity to use any variety of vegetables you like and to clean out the fridge from ripening veggies and leftovers.

You may use a variety of other veggies like eggplant, zucchini, peppers, chilies, rice, beans, mushrooms, tofu, seitan, tempeh, etc.

Mexican Lasagna

 40 minutes   4 -6 servings

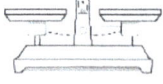
16 tortillas (corn or wheat) or 5-6 large wraps
1 pound sweet potatoes (or regular potatoes, or squash)
1 large onion
½ pepper
1 rib celery
2 carrots
3 cloves garlic
½ cup beans (any bean)
½ cup corn
2 handfuls of chopped kale of spinach
1 teaspoon salt
hot sauce (as much as you like)
1 quart tomato sauce or salsa
5 to 10 sprigs cilantro

1 pack of tofu
2 teaspoons lemon juice
1 tablespoon Dijon mustard
2 cloves of garlic
1 teaspoon salt
1 cup of water (half a cup if you are using silken tofu)

Mexican Lasagna

Mexican Lasagna is not a thing in Mexico or Italy. It is something we invented in America to offend Mexicans and Italians in equal proportion.

The beauty of it, other than being delicious, is that it's super-easy and you don't have to worry about the cooking of the whole-wheat lasagna pasta. You may use any type of tortillas or wraps for this: corn, whole-wheat gluten-free, etc. To make it Tex-Mex, replace the tomato sauce with Barbecue sauce, or make it half and half: tomato/BBQ.

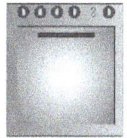 Preheat the oven to 325°. Dice the onions, pepper, carrot, celery, sweet potatoes, and garlic and roast in the oven for ~15 minutes. If you have other leftover veggies in the fridge or freezer, don't be shy about it, throw it in.

While the veggies roast, blend the tofu and seasoning in the second portion of the recipe for the tofu cream. Savory Cashew Cream *(page 32)* will work fine too.

Add all veggies to the bowl, along with ¼ cup of tomato sauce, salt, hot sauce and about ½ of the cilantro, chopped, and mix well. If you have a preferred seasoning mix, like lemon pepper, Old Bay or Mexican Seasoning, you may add it too.

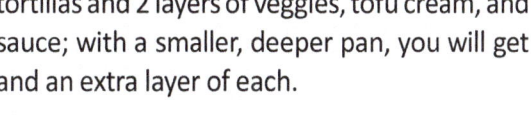

Use a baking pan that is 6-14" long, 6-10" wide and 2-4" deep. With a larger and shallower pan, you 7008will get 3 layers of tortillas and 2 layers of veggies, tofu cream, and sauce; with a smaller, deeper pan, you will get and an extra layer of each.

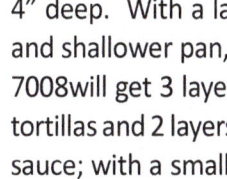

Spread a bit of tomato sauce at the bottom, and lay the first layer of tortilla/wrap. Cut the tortillas (or wraps) to fit the baking pan. It doesn't matter if it overlays or if it doesn't fit perfectly, it will not be noticeable. Then, depending on how many layers you are planning, cover the tortillas with half or one third of the veggies, and then cover the vegetables with one third or one fourth of the tomato sauce and tofu cream (you will need to spare a bit to garnish the top of the lasagna). Repeat the procedure for the next one or two layers. Then apply the last layer of tortillas and cover it with the remaining tomato sauce.

Use the remainder of the tofu cream to decorate with stripes or random patterns.

Bake for about 15-20 minutes at 350°.

Garnish with the chopped cilantro or green onions and serve.

Other Ingredients: you may use a variety of other veggies like eggplant, zucchini, peppers, chilies, or add rice, other beans, mushrooms, tofu, seitan, tempeh, etc.

Stuffed Cabbage

 40 minutes 10 rolls

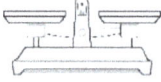
1 large cabbage of any kind
3-4 cups of cooked rice
1 onion
4 mushrooms
1 zucchini or squash
1 pepper
1 rib celery
3 cloves garlic
1 to 2 teaspoons salt or the Easy Veggies Seasoning *(page 19)*.
¼ teaspoon cumin
¼ teaspoon of garlic powder
One pint of tomato sauce

Stuffed Cabbage with Creamy Tomato Sauce

Stuffed leaves are versatile and a great use for leftovers. You can use cabbage, grape leaves or collards greens (remove stems). Cabbage is easiest. You may also use a variety of combinations of veggies and starches, like faro, bulgur, potato, etc.

 Preheat the oven to 350° and start boiling water in a large pan.

Small dice the onions, pepper, celery, squash and mushrooms, and mince the garlic. Season the veggies with salt and garlic powder or use the Easy Veggies Seasoning *(page 19)*, then roast the veggies until they are nicely tanned, about 10-15 minutes. Leave the oven on.

While the veggies roast, carefully peel 10-15 leaves of cabbage and dip them in salted simmering water for about 5-10 minutes, to soft them, then strain. If the leaves break a bit as you peel, you'll be able to disguise it when you roll them up.

Mix the rice and roasted veggies in a bowl with ½ cup of tomato sauce, and your preferred spices or seasoning mix.

Use 2 generous spoonfuls of the filling over the leaf, then fold it, sides in first, then lengthwise. Trim the stem if it is too hard to fold. Place them on a casserole or baking sheet, seam down. Use the remainder of the tomato sauce over the rolls. Bake in the oven for about 10-15 minutes, until nicely tanned.

Other Ingredients: you may use a variety of other veggies like eggplant, zucchini, peppers, chilies, other beans, mushrooms, tofu, seitan, tempeh, etc.

You may use most of the sauces in this book, instead of the tomato sauce, such as the Mushroom Gravy *(page 44)*, Zesty Tahini *(page 21)*, Creamy Tomato *(page 47)*, Mild Curry *(page 50)*, Hollandaise *(page 28)*, Spicy Peanut *(page 42)*, Mushroom Gravy *(page 44)*, or Cauliflower Cheese *(page 52)*.

Nice touch: Since the veggies will produce a good amount of moisture, sprinkle breadcrumbs or oats around, over and between the rolls and tomato sauce. They will absorb moisture and flavor.

Gnocchi with Pesto

 20 minutes   2-3 servings

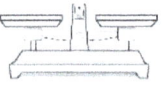
1 pack of whole wheat gnocchi (1 pound)
½ cup to 1 cup Mild Pesto *(page 49)*
1 cup peas
½ onion
1 red pepper

Many supermarkets offer whole wheat gnocchi. They contain potatoes, whole wheat flour, and other starches. Most are egg-free. They are as versatile as pasta and can be cooked with a variety of sauces and vegetable combinations.

Boil salted water in a large pot. Add the gnocchi as soon as the water boils.

It is very easy to know when the gnocchi is ready because they float when they a fully cooked. If whole wheat, let it cook 5 minutes longer, then strain.

Dice and roast the pepper and onion while the gnocchi cooks.

If using frozen peas, add them to the boiling water just as the gnocchi is fully cooked.

Strain the gnocchi, mix with the sauce and veggies in the pan. Add a bit of water if necessary, and serve.

Gnocchi with pesto

Everyday Bowl

 30 minutes   4 servings

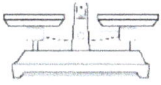
1-2 cups rice
2 Tablespoons corn, beans or chickpeas
½ cup broccoli and/or kale and/or spinach
2 Tablespoons mushroom
2 Tablespoons peppers
2 Tablespoons sweet potato or carrot
4 oz baked tofu or 2 Tablespoons frozen peas
One of our sauces (pages 21- 52)

My best advice is to choose one day of the week to roast a bunch of veggies in a large batch and store them in the fridge, in separate containers, or even all together, if you like your bowls tossed. Roasted veggies in safe fridge temperature (under 40°) should last one week. Same advice for cooking a large batch of rice.

Everyday Bowl with Red Curry

The easiest way is to roast all veggies in the oven, but a pan works too.

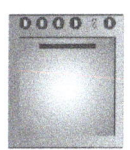 Preheat the oven to 350° or a pan to medium-high. Dice and slice all large veggies, break broccoli into bite-size pieces (stems are perfectly edible too, or you may save them for making a soup) and season them with salt and garlic powder and/or your favorite spice mix. Add the corn and seasoned tofu, and roast until nicely browned, about 10-15 minutes. The broccoli may start burning before the other veggies, so you may add it later or pull it out first. Serve over the rice, with your favorite sauce.

 You really can't go wrong with adding avocado or guacamole to a bowl.

Everyday Salads

Salads have no rules. They are whatever you like and whatever you have in the fridge. My advice is to have a couple of our dressings always available, which is half of the effort for having a delicious salad, and to balance dark leafy greens, red veggies, legumes, a starch component, crunchy and filling vegetables, nuts and seeds, and perhaps plant-based protein. The following are some combination ideas, for you to mix and match.

Black Eyed Peas

 30 minutes  2 servings

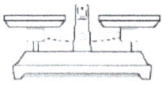
3-4 handfuls spring mix or any greens or cabbage
1 can black-eyed peas
1 large tomato
2-3 ribs of celery
1 bell pepper
¼ of a large onion
1-2 cloves garlic
1 Tablespoon lemon juice or vinegar
1 teaspoon hot sauce
1 teaspoon salt

This works well as a salsa, over a bed of greens, over a toast or for scooping with chips. Dice all veggies small, about 1/4", mince the garlic and toss with the seasoning in a bowl, and serve over the greens.

Other Ingredients: works very well adding or replacing mangoes or avocados. A couple of sprigs of cilantro is a nice touch. If you like it hot, fresh hot peppers work great. Add any other veggies you enjoy or have in the fridge.

Garden Caesar

 15-20 minutes   2 servings

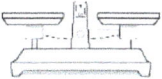
3-4 handfuls spinach or any greens or cabbage
1 cucumber
1 carrot
1 pepper
¼ onion
1 can corn
1 tomato
1 handful Soy Curls ™ (optional)
1 cup Caesar Dressing *(page 25)*

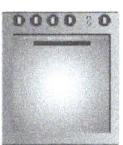
Soak the Soy Curls™ in water with 2-4 Tablespoons of soy sauce and/or some spice mix like Old Bay or lemon pepper, for about ½ hour, then strain and roast in the oven at 325° until tanned, about 15 minutes.

If you don't have time to soak the Soy Curls™, you can do it in a pan: set the heat to medium, add ½ cup of water and 2-4 Tablespoon of soy sauce, add the Soy Curls™ and put the lid on. Once it dries, see if they feel tender. If still dry, add more water. Once tender, let the water evaporate completely, then start roasting them until they tan and are light brown on the sides.

While the Soy Curls™ roast, dice the pepper and onions to medium size, about 1/2". Slice or dice the cucumber and tomato. Shred the carrot. Toss the veggies with the corn, Soy Curls™ and dressing, and serve over the greens. I like my spinach sliced thin (chiffonade).

Garden Caesar

Other Ingredients: works fine with tofu, seitan or just avocados. Add any other veggies you like or have in the fridge.

Strawberries Field

 15 minutes 2-4 servings

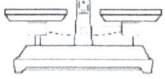

3-4 handfuls spinach or any greens or cabbage
~10 strawberries
2 mandarins or oranges
¼ cup walnuts
2 slices bread
½ pack tofu
1 cup Ginger Sesame Dressing *(page 38)* **or Balsamic Vinaigrette** *(36)* **or Balsamic Gastrique** *(37)*.

Cut the tofu in cubes of ~ ½", then soak in water with ~4 Tablespoons of soy sauce and/or a spice mix like Old Bay or lemon pepper, for about ½ hour. Then strain and roast in the oven at 325° until tanned, about 15 minutes.

If you don't have time to soak the tofu, toss it in a bowl with 2 tablespoons of soy sauce and just a little bit of water, to help the soy sauce move around the tofu bits easily. While the tofu roasts, cut the slices of bread into crouton-size pieces and place them onto another baking sheet. Season them with a bit of salt and garlic powder or the Easy Veggies Seasoning (page 19) and pop it in the oven with the tofu for the last 5 minutes, until crunchy.

Meanwhile, slice the strawberries and break down the tangerines, halving each pulled piece. Then mix the fruits, walnut, tofu, and dressing in a bowl, and serve over the greens, whole or sliced thin (chiffonade).

Other Ingredients: You may make candied walnuts for this: mix the walnuts with 2 tablespoons of sugar, a sprinkle of cinnamon, ginger and nutmeg and a ½ tablespoon of water, then spread them on a baking sheet and roast until they are nicely tanned. They will crisp up when they chill. The timing is a bit tricky; ~15 minutes at 350°, but keep an eye on them. It's a small margin of error between golden and burnt. Add any other veggies you like or have in the fridge.

Quinoa Tabbouleh

25 minutes   4 servings

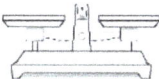

2 cups of quinoa
4 cups of water
1-2 teaspoons of salt
1 cucumber
2 tomatoes
½ onion
1-2 garlic cloves
5-10 sprigs of parsley
Handful of finely sliced spinach
3 Tablespoon of lemon juice
½ to 1 cup of olives and/or capers (optional, delicious)

I am a huge fan of Tabbouleh, but I'm often overwhelmed by the parsley. I have found it more pleasant when I replace some of the parsley with spinach. I am also passionate about olives (except for the horrible cheap black stuff that comes in cans), and I believe they absolutely complete the Tabbouleh. You are welcome to make it with the traditional bulgur. The quinoa is a nice and nutritious touch, which also makes it a gluten-free option.

Tabbouleh

Bring the quinoa to boil in salted water and simmer for ~15 to 20 minutes. Let it chill. Meanwhile, dice the onion, cucumber, tomatoes, and olives, mince the garlic and thin slice the parsley and spinach.

Mix the veggies with the seasoning and quinoa once it chilled.

Other Ingredients: Tabbouleh typically does not have a large assortment of veggies in it, but nothing is stopping you from adding whatever you have in the fridge, freezer or pantry. Just do not let a Lebanese person see it. Some options are avocado, peppers, peas, shredded carrot, celery, and radish.

Power Grains

 20 minutes   2 servings

¼ cabbage or any greens
1 large carrot
5-10 radishes
¼ large onion
½ pepper (of any color)
½ can corn
1-2 cups cooked quinoa *(page 55)*
1 cup seitan *(page 124, or baked tofu 125)*
½ cup oats
1 cup Zesty Tahini *(page 21)*

Thin slice the onion and cabbage, shred the carrot and radishes and toss with all other ingredients and dressing in a large bowl.

Other Ingredients: You may use several types of grain for this, faro, barley, wheat berries, millet, or anything else you feel adventurous to try.

Replacing the seitan with avocados, chickpeas or beans works well.

My Sweet Kale

 15 minutes   2-4 servings

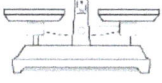
½ bunch kale or any greens or cabbage
¼ onion
1 carrot
1 cup cooked quinoa and/or 1 can chickpeas
½ cup dried cranberries or raisins
2 ribs celery, diced
1 cup shelled edamame
Balsamic Vinaigrette *(36)* **or Balsamic Gastrique** *(37)*

My Sweet Kale

Pull the kale leaves off the stem, slice it thin with a knife or through the slicing disk of a food processor. Literally, massage it in a bowl with a bit of lemon for a couple of minutes. Add thin sliced or diced onion, shredded carrot and all other ingredients and toss.

Other Ingredients: You may use a variety of veggies, like avocados, tomato, corn, peas, etc. You may replace the cranberries or raisins with fresh fruits, like apples or strawberries. If you are not into kale, spinach or spring mix is just fine.

Tuna Beet

 20 minutes  2-4 servings

2-4 large beets
2-4 handfuls spinach
1 tomato
¼ onion
1 carrot
2 Tablespoons sunflower seeds
½ recipe Chickpea Tuna Salad *(page 120)*
1 cup Ranch Dressing *(page 27)*

 Fill a medium-sized pan ½ way with salted water and put on the stove to boil.

Rinse, scrub and slice the beets, about ¼" thick, and place in the pot. Let it simmer until tender to the fork, about 15 minutes. You may also roast it in the oven, for about 15-20 minutes at 325°.

Meanwhile, slice the tomato and onion and shred the carrot.

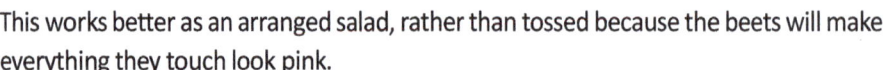

This works better as an arranged salad, rather than tossed because the beets will make everything they touch look pink.

Make a bed with the spinach; arrange the slices of tomato, then beets, then and onions. Then scoop the "tuna" salad and sprinkle it all with the shredded carrots and sunflower seeds.

Other Ingredients: You may use several other veggies, like avocados, peppers, corn, peas, etc.

You may replace the "tuna" salad with chickpeas, beans, avocados or corn.

 You really can't go wrong with adding avocado or guacamole to a sala

Pesto Pasta

 15 minutes   2-4 servings

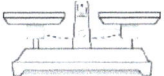
2 cups cooked whole wheat pasta (I like fusilli)
¼ onion
1 tomato
1 pepper (equivalent in mixed colors even better!)
1 rib celery
~ 5 olives
¼ cup Mild Pesto *(page 49)*

While you cook the pasta in salted water, dice the onion, tomato, pepper, celery, and olives.

Strain and rinse the pasta in cold water, to cool, and toss with the veggies and Pesto.

Pesto Pasta

Other Ingredients: You may use a variety of veggies: cucumber, zucchini, eggplant, edamame, etc. If you came across some beautiful, ripe and colorful tomatoes, you may use just them, like in the picture.

Nice Touch: Baked Tofu *(page 125)* matches well with this salad.

Tofu "Egg" Salad

 30 minutes   2-4 servings

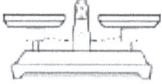
1 pack of tofu (12-16oz, regular or silken)
2 cloves garlic
1 teaspoon salt
¼ teaspoon turmeric (optional)
½ onion
3 ribs celery (also works beautifully with broccoli)
~ ½ cup Mayo *(page 22)*

Tofu "Egg" Salad

Tofu "Egg" Salad is easy and versatile; excellent for salads, sandwiches and as a spread. If you have time, like many other tofu recipes, this works best if you cook slowly at a mid temperature. It allows for the tofu to dehydrate and form a nicer texture.

Preheat a pan to medium, or the oven at 300°. The pan is fine, but the oven is more efficient for larger batches. The oven often forms a better texture and you don't need to keep stirring it.

If using a pan over the stove, preheat the pan on medium and use your hands, crumble the tofu into the pan. Add minced garlic and spread the seasoning. Toss and mix well.

While the tofu roasts, dice the onions and celery, mince the garlic and slice the mushrooms. Add all veggies to a pot and roast them slightly before adding the tofu, so to remove some of the moisture. Works better to cook slowly, at medium, stirring occasionally and gently not to mash the crumbles. If you stir and flip too often, you won't allow a nice roasting crust to form on the tofu. You may speed it up, by cranking up to mid-high, stirring a bit more frequently. About 15 minutes.

If using the oven, mix the hand crumbled tofu with the veggies and seasoning and, lay it on a baking sheet or pan and roast at 300-325°. It is ready when the tofu starts to brown, forming a nice crust, about 15-20 minutes.

Once the tofu is roasted, mix with the diced raw veggies and the mayo.

Regular or silken tofu is a matter of personal preference for texture.

Other Ingredients: You may use many different veggies in this recipe. I prefer raw crunchier veggies, like diced broccoli, cauliflower, zucchini, carrots or radishes.

Everyday Sandwiches

As for salads, sandwiches have no rules. They are whatever you like and what veggies and ingredients you have in the fridge. My advice is to have a couple of our dressings always available, like Mayo *(page 22)*, Tartar *(page 23)*, Thousand Island *(page 24)*, Ginger Sesame *(page 38)* or Cilantro *(page 26)*. The dressing is half the effort for a delicious sandwich. As long as you have a good dressing, even just spinach, tomato and onions will suffice. The following are some combination ideas for you to mix and match:

Avocado Joy

 15 minutes

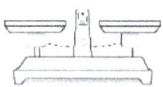

1 whole wheat roll
½ avocado
1 tomato
¼ small onion
Handful spinach
½ carrot
1 radish
Zesty Tahini *(page21)*

Slice the avocado, tomato, onion, and shred the carrot and radish.

Arrange the spinach and veggies on the roll. Sprinkle a bit of sea salt and top with a generous amount of sauce.

Other Ingredients: works very well adding or replacing pickles, jalapenos, beets or even mangoes. A couple of sprigs of cilantro is a nice touch. I love it with arugula or watercress, instead of the spinach. Any other of our dressings will work.

Portobello

 15 minutes

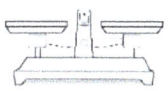
1 whole wheat bun
1 Portobello cap
½ onion
3 slices tomato
2 shredded kale leaves
1-2 Tablespoons Balsamic Vinaigrette *(page 36)*
Zesty Tahini *(page 21)*, **Mild Pesto** *(page 49)* **or**
Spicy Peanut *(page 42)*

Even at French Culinary school, a chef told me he'd take a grilled Portobello over a beef burger, anytime.

Sliced babybello mushrooms with Pesto

 Preheat the oven to 350° or a pan to medium-high.

Rinse well the Portobello cap or any other mushroom, remove the stem, and place the cap in the pan. Slice ½ of a small onion and add it to the pan. Then thin slice a couple of kale leaves and add it last to the pan and sprinkle with a bit of sea salt, garlic powder and/or the Easy Veggies Seasoning *(page 19)*. Do a similar process if you are using an oven.

The Portobello and onion will roast in about the same time; 6-10 minutes in a pan, 12-15 minutes in the oven. The kale just needs some 2-5 minutes to soften.

Toward the end, use the pan or oven to warm up the bun. Assemble and enjoy.

Other Ingredients: works well adding or replacing pickles, jalapenos, avocado, roasted peppers, and shredded carrots. An olive tapenade hits the jackpot.

Easy Reuben

 15 minutes

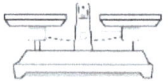

1 whole wheat roll
½ to 1 cup of Seitan *(page 124)*, **or Baked Tofu**
(page 125)
¼ small onion
1/8 of a cabbage (red will look nice)
¼ carrot
¼ cup Thousand Island
~5 slices of pickles
½ avocado (optional, for deliciousness)

This is a much healthier version of the classic. I can't find in my heart the love for sauerkraut, so, for me the fresh cabbage to be a plus.

Easy Ruben

Thin slice the cabbage and onion and shred the carrot. Toss it with some of the Thousand Islands to bind it together. You may use cold seitan; if, like me, you prefer it warm, thinly slice the seitan or tofu onto a pan, seasoning it with a touch of soy sauce, or Easy Veggies Seasoning *(page 19)*. Do a similar process if you are using an oven.

Arrange the veggies on the roll, top with the seitan or tofu and finish with the remainder of the Thousand Island.

Philly "Steak"

 15 minutes

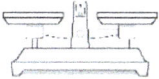

1 whole wheat roll
½ onion
½ pepper
2-3 mushrooms
½ cup baked tofu, seitan or Soy Curls™
¼ cup **Cauliflower Cheese Sauce** *(page 52)*, **Spicy Peanut** *(42)*, **BBQ** *(29)*, **Tomato Sauce** *(46)*, **Mild Curry** *(50)* or **Red Pepper Coulis** *(43)*

This is based on the staple from my adopted hometown, minus 600 calories. If you have access to seitan or just made a great batch of Seitan *(page 124*, this is a delicious way to enjoy it.

Preheat the oven to 350° or a pan to medium-high.

Cut the onion and peppers in ½" dice and the mushroom in ¼" slices, and place it in the pan or oven. Then thinly slice the seitan, and sprinkle with a bit of sea salt, garlic powder, soy sauce, and/or the Easy Veggies Seasoning *(page 19)* and add it to the pan or oven. Roast all for ~10-15 minutes.

Toward the end, use the pan or oven to warm up the roll.

Other Ingredients: Avocados are a natural replacement for the fat and creaminess of cheese.

Melanzana (Eggplant)

 15 minutes

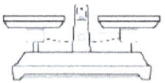
1 whole wheat roll or bun
3-4 slices Roasted Eggplant *(page 140)*
1 tomato
½ small onion
Handful spinach or a leaf of kale
¼ cup Red Pepper Coulis *(page 43)* **or Tomato Sauce** *(page 46)*

There's a good reason an eggplant sandwich is a staple of every corner Italian place. A crispy roasted eggplant sandwich is a thing of beauty.

 Preheat the oven to 350 or a pan on medium-high. Cut the onion in ¼" and add it to the pan or oven, then add the eggplant to reheat, then cut the kale in very thin slices and add it too. While this heats, cut the tomato in ¼" slices.

Add the bun or roll to ride along with the veggies for a couple of minutes to crisp up.

Arrange all veggies on the roll or bun, and top with a generous amount of the Red Pepper Coulis or tomato sauce, hot or cold.

Other Ingredients: Many veggies work well in this sandwich and can be added or replaced: Avocados, beets, pepper, zucchini, sweet potato, and squash.

Meatball Sandwich

 You may use this same recipe for a fantastic vegan Meatball Sandwich, replacing the eggplant with the Tofu Meatballs *(page 126)*.

Fresh Veggies

 15 minutes

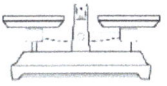
1 whole wheat roll, bun or sliced bread
1 tomato
¼ onion
½ carrot
4-5 slices of beets (or ½ avocado)
Handful spinach
4-5 slices of kosher pickles
Ranch Dressing *(page 27)*

Sometimes, all you need are some fresh veggies and a nice dressing for a perfect summer lunch.

If you are cooking the beets, rather than using canned, start with that. Bring salted water to boil, add the beets to the water at any time and simmer until tender to the fork, about 15 minutes. Strain them, and let them chill for a moment. You can also bake in the oven for ~15 minutes at 325°.

While the beets cook, slice the tomato and onions in ¼" slices, and shred the carrot. Arrange all the veggies on a roll, bun, or sliced bread and top with a generous amount of Ranch Dressing.

Other Ingredients: If all you have in the fridge is onion, tomato, and cucumber, it will do, the dressing will make up for the rest.

You may use mung bean sprouts, radish, kale, pickles, peppers, cucumber, mushrooms, tofu, etc.

 And, as always, you really can't go wrong with adding avocado or guacamole to a sandwich.

Darn Good BLT

 30 minutes

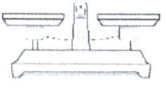 **4-6 slices of tempeh bacon** *(page 129)*
Handful spinach
½ tomato
½ avocado (optional)
¼ small onion (optional)
Ranch Dressing (optional – *page 27***)**

BLT with tempeh bacon, spinach, tomato, avocado and ranch dressing

Simply delicious, a few ingredients that work in perfect harmony.

Roast the tempeh per the Tempeh recipe *(page 129)*. Then slice the tomatoes and avocados. Add the spinach and sauce.

Other Ingredients:

We favor dark leaves like spinach, kale, arugula or watercress, but you can use any lettuce or even cabbage.

As we mention in the tempeh recipe, we may also make "bacon" with eggplant, mushroom or tofu.

Many sauces will work well, including Mayo *(page 22)*, Cilantro *(26)*, Thousand Island *(24)*, Caesar *(25)*, Zesty Tahini *(21)* or Tartar *(23)*.

Easy Banh Mi

 10 minutes

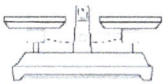
1 whole wheat roll
1/3 carrot
2 radishes
6-8 slices cucumber
1 slice onion
½ cup Baked Tofu *(page 125)*
6-10 slices pickles
1/3 cup Cilantro Dressing *(page 26)*
2 sprigs cilantro

Easy Banh Mi with Baked Tofu

 Shred the carrot and radish, slice the cucumber, slice the onion and break it down, and then arrange all ingredients on the roll. Ideally, we'd pickle the carrots and radish, but in this quick version, we are using the dill/kosher pickles to bring that flavor. I like it with lots of cilantro dressing.

Easy Bean Burger

 30 minutes   6 patties

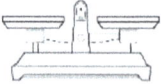
1 can of beans of any kind

½ onion

3 cloves garlic or 1 Tablespoon garlic powder

1 carrot

½ pepper of any color

¾ to 1 cup vital wheat flour (better texture), whole wheat flour or a gluten free flour of your choice

½ teaspoon cumin

1 teaspoon salt

1-2 Tablespoons soy sauce or tamari

Red Kidney Bean Burger in a whole wheat Kaiser roll

There are many ways of making bean burgers; this one is possibly the simplest.

Rinse and drain the beans thoroughly, let sit in the strainer for a bit to dry. Then add them with everything else to a food processor, and pulse all ingredients into a chunky dough. It's a nicer effect when small bits of the veggies are still visible, rather than having it all fully blended into a paste. If you happen to have a grinder, it's an even better tool.

Add more flour of any kind, or drizzle a bit of water if necessary to adjust the texture. We are looking for a consistent chunky dough that is just dry enough to be formed into patties and hold the shape but not too dry that it will not be appetizing. If you happen to have molds (3-5" in diameter and a ~½ inch deep), they will be perfect.

Preheat a pan to medium or the oven to 325°. Scoop the dough and form a ball in your hands, a bit bigger than a golf ball, then press into a patty on the pan or on a baking sheet for the oven. Roast until nicely browned in the pan ~3-5 minutes each side, or in the oven for 15-20 minutes.

If you baked in the oven, the patties will release better after they chill a bit. Serve with your favorite burger fixings.

Other ingredients: You may replace or add other veggies to the burger; it's an excellent use for mushroom, kale or broccoli stems. Just add a bit more seasoning and flour as you add more veggies.

Instead of the flour, you may use other starches, like bread slices, potatoes, oats, quinoa, couscous, polenta or cooked rice. Just look for a dough consistency firm enough that you can form into a patty.

Mushrooms will bring a "meaty" flavor to the burger.

A few drops of liquid smoke add a nice touch to the flavor.

If you are into a "bloody" burger look, add a few slices of beet.

Nice Touch: <u>This recipe will turn out significantly better if you use dry beans, lentils or chickpeas instead of canned</u>: Soak half a pound of any type of beans for at least 4 hours before using in this recipe. Drain, and use instead of the can of beans. In such case, you may need a bit less flour.

If using dry legumes, you will want to be sure the burgers cook thoroughly, because the taste of uncooked beans, lentils or chickpeas is awful. It will work better in the over, in burger molds, for ~20 minutes at 325°.

Chickpea "Tuna" Salad

 20 minutes   4-6 servings

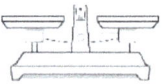
- 1 can of chickpeas
- 1 sheet nori
- ¼ cup capers with brine
- ½ onion
- 1 rib celery
- ½ Tablespoon Dijon mustard
- ½ to 1 cup Mayo *(page 22)*
- 1 Tablespoon lemon juice
- 1 teaspoon nutritional yeast
- 1 Tablespoon relish
- 1 teaspoon salt

Chickpea "Tuna" Salad sandwich, with cucumber and tomato

 Rinse the chickpeas on a strainer and let dry a bit. Then pulse a few times in a food processor, stirring in between. The goal is to keep it chunky, not to make the chickpeas entirely into a paste. Mince the onions and celery, and mix all the ingredients in a bowl. Alternatively, lightly mash the chickpeas with a fork and then combine all the ingredients in a bowl.

Other ingredients: you may use nuts, like walnuts, in addition to or instead of chickpeas. It will be a richer and more caloric recipe.

Add olives.

Nice Touch: this will taste better if you use dry chickpeas. Soak chickpeas overnight or for at least 4 hours. Put them in a pot with water seasoned with salt, bring to boil, and simmer for 20-30 minutes.

For the sandwich, just tomatoes and cucumber compose it well. To make it super-special, arugula or watercress are a beautiful touch.

Roasted Veggies Wrap

🕐 25 minutes   2 wraps

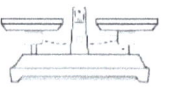

¼ onion
1 pepper
½ tomato
8 oz sweet potato or butternut squash
4 mushrooms
6 oz spinach or coleslaw
6 oz tofu, seitan or tempeh (optional)
2 whole wheat wraps
one of our dressings

Roasted Veggies Wrap with Ginger Sesame dressing

Wraps are another excellent opportunity to use leftover vegetables: tomato, mushroom, peppers, kale, sweet potatoes, squash, corn, beans, peas, string beans, etc. As long as you have a good dressing, even just spinach, tomato and onions suffice.

Preheat the oven to 350º. Slice the veggies, season them with salt, garlic powder and/or your favorite spice mix and roast them until browned, ~10 minutes. No need to roast the tomato, use it raw. If using tofu, slice it in ¼" slices, pour a bit of soy sauce on it and roast it along with the veggies.

Place a generous amount of the roasted veggies, tomato and spinach/slaw in the center of wrap. If it's a, smaller, 6-10" wrap, you may want to do it open-ended on both or one end. If it is a larger 10-12" wrap, it will be easier to fold both sides; it takes a bit of practice, but this is how you do it: fold both laterals of the wraps about 1/3 of the way in, hold these laterals with your pinkies, while you grab the bottom part of the wrap and roll over the filling, squeezing the filling toward yourself, and then finish rolling over.

Many sauces will work well, including Mayo *(page 22)*, Cilantro *(26)*, Thousand Island *(24)*, Caesar *(25)*, Zesty Tahini *(21)*, Ginger Sesame *(38)* or Tartar *(23)*.

Nice Touch:

Keep the oven on, and toast the rolled wraps for a few minutes. The wrap itself will taste better. Or you may toast it in a pan or a panini press.

You really can't go wrong with adding avocado or guacamole to a wrap.

Fillings, Sides, Spreads, Bites

Seitan

 120 minutes (30 minutes hands-on)  ~2 pounds of finished seitan

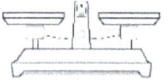
2 cups vital wheat flour
1 ½ cups of water
2 Tablespoons soy sauce or tamari
1 teaspoon nutritional yeast
1 teaspoon garlic powder
1 teaspoon onion powder
1 teaspoon paprika
1 teaspoon salt
1 teaspoon raw sugar

Another ¼ cup soy sauce for simmering
1 sheet of nori

Artisanal seitan is made with high-gluten whole wheat bread flour, and the dough requires intensive kneading and rinsing. It does not fit the purpose of this book, so we are suggesting an easier version, with vital wheat, pure gluten flour.

Seitan, shredded and roasted

Mix all the dry ingredients in a mixer with the hook attachment, or in a bowl with a spatula, then add the water and knead the dough. It should feel like a springy, rubbery pizza dough and should come off your hands. It may, at this point, look like you imagine baboon brains would look like. Don't worry about that.

Notice: after the kneading, gluten will get rigid, and the dough will need to rest before cooking. Let it sit for at least 20 minutes.

After letting the dough rest, break the dough in 4 or 5 smaller pieces to better absorb the flavor. Put the dough in a large pot with enough water to cover it. Add ¼ cup of soy sauce and one sheet of nori, shredded. Bring it to a simmer, turn down to low, and simmer for about an hour. Then you may strain it for final roasting or cooking, or just store it in the refrigerator in that same broth, until you are ready to use it.

Other ingredients: a ¼ teaspoon of cumin and another teaspoon of paprika in the simmering water works well, but the taste of cumin may interfere with other recipes you may want to use the seitan for. You may add a few slices of beet to the pot to color the seitan a bit meatier.

Once simmered, you have edible seitan, but it's still too moist to be enjoyable. The next step is highly recommended.

Additional Seasoning and Roasting:
- **1 pound seitan**
- **2 teaspoons Braggs Aminos or tamari or soy sauce**
- **1 teaspoon raw sugar**

The goal at this point is to remove the excess moisture and give it a bit of crispiness. The easiest way is to use the oven, with the seitan shredded with the slicing blade of a food processor. Instead of a food processor, you can cut the seitan with a knife in any shape. Note that the larger the chunks, the harder to remove excess moisture. For larger cuts, give the seitan a good hand squeeze first, and then cook at lower temperatures.

Preheat the oven to 275- 325° or a pan to medium. Toss the seitan with the seasoning. Meat has a natural sweetness to it, and this is why we add a bit of sugar to replicate the flavor depth and umaminess. Barbecue Sauce *(page 29)* works great for this purpose.

If using the oven, spread the seitan well over a tray, or make kebabs and roast for about 15 min until it gets crispy. If it got a bit too crispy, no worries, it will be just fine. It will rehydrate nicely in whichever sauce you use to cook, toss or brush with. In fact, it's hard to think of a sauce or dressing it won't taste good in.

Seitan kebabs brushed with BBQ sauce

Tofu Meatball

 60 minutes (if you let it set)  4 servings

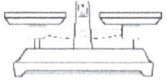
1 package extra firm tofu
4 mushrooms
~5 garlic cloves
3 to 6 slices of whole wheat bread (depends on the tofu and the bread)
2 to 3 Tablespoons tamari or soy sauce
1 Tablespoon ground flax seeds (optional)
5-10 drops liquid smoke (optional)

This is one of the easiest among many recipes of plant-based "meatballs". It works well and has a great consistency. It's best when you let it set by allowing it to chill completely, thus the longer prep time above.

Spaghetti & Meatballs, with tomato sauce

Preheat the oven to 300-320°. Strain the tofu and give it a squeeze to expel moisture. Put all ingredients in the food processor, and mix well. A grinder also works. A blender will be fine with a bit of patience to stop often to push things down and then scoop it out.

 Adjust the consistency with more or fewer bread slices, if needed. We are looking for a dough that is just dry enough that you can roll into balls in your hands and that will hold its shape, but not too dry that won't be enjoyable. Scoop a large tablespoon onto your hands, form balls just a bit smaller than a golf ball, and lay them on a non-stick baking sheet (or brush a small amount of oil). Not much distance is needed; the balls will neither rise nor shrink. Bake for 25-30 minutes, until they are nicely browned. Then let cool completely before reheating in whichever sauce you prefer.

Other Ingredients: You may add a few other veggies to the dough, like kale, spinach, beet, onion, etc. Just adjust the consistency with bread slices and add a bit more salt or soy sauce.

You may replace the bread with other starches, like potato, rice or oats, adjusting the consistency to a dough that you can form into a ball.

Tip: Double the batch for future dishes or a Meatball Sandwich *(114)*.

Tofu Meatloaf

The Tofu Meatballs recipe will work for a Meatloaf. We suggest you add a few ingredients for a special occasion meatloaf:

After you already ran the food processor with the meatball recipe, add 1 tablespoon of baking powder, ½ cup of nuts, ¼ cup of olives, ¼ cup of chopped sundried tomatoes and ¼ onion, Pulse the processor a few times to chop, but not entirely destroy these ingredients. Or you may use about ½ cup of random minced veggies.

 Preheat the oven to 300-325°. Use a non-stick bread baking pan or brush a bit of oil. Bake for ~30 minutes, until it's nicely browned. It is best to let it cool completely before removing from the pan, so, for a special occasion, cook the day before, to be safe, and reheat in the oven.

Works well with Tomato Sauce *(page 46)* or Mushroom Gravy *(page 44)*.

Quinoa Caviar

 25 minutes

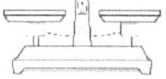
1 cup quinoa
3 cups water
4 sheets nori (or any dark colored seaweed)
1 Tablespoon salt
2 Tablespoons lemon juice
1 teaspoon vinegar

This one is not for those with high blood pressure, since it is pretty salty, to resemble caviar.

Blend the seaweed with the water and seasoning, then use it to cook the quinoa, about 20 minutes. The quinoa shouldn't absorb all the water. You want it to be a bit moist, not entirely dry, so add more water if needed.

Quinoa Caviar with a drizzle of Zesty Tahini

Let it chill in the fridge before serving.

Serve with toast, crackers or chips, garnish with a bit of very mildly salted **Cashew Cream** *(page 30)*, **Zesty Tahini** *(page 21),* or **Mayo** *(page 22)*.

Tempeh Bacon

 25 minutes 4-6 servings

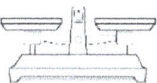
1 pack (12-16oz) tempeh
¼ cup soy sauce
1 cup to 1 pint of water (depends on your container for soaking)
1 Tablespoon raw sugar or maple syrup
2 garlic cloves
Pinch of cumin
1 teaspoon salt
10 drops liquid smoke (optional, for smoky flavor)

Tempeh Bacon

For those who like the salty, smoky, and slightly sweet taste of bacon.

Of all texturized vegetable proteins and meat substitutes, tempeh is the one I find more challenging to work with. However, tempeh can taste great and is very nutritious. The most essential concept is that tempeh must marinate. Otherwise, it will be very dry and crumbly.

Making tempeh from scratch is a long and artisanal process that involves cooking and fermenting soybeans. This is out of the scope of this book.

Cut the tempeh in ¼ inch slices and marinate overnight, or for at least one hour, in enough water and seasoning to cover the slices.

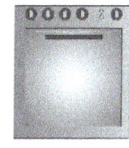

Preheat the oven to 300?-325 or a pan on medium-high. Lay the slices on a baking sheet or pan, and pour some of the marinating liquid over the slices. Roast it to a nice brown, about 10-20 minutes in the oven, or 5-10 minutes in a pan.

Other ingredients: This same recipe can be used for making "bacon" from mushrooms, coconut or eggplant. Let thin slices marinate, then roast in the oven at 275-300° until crispy, ~30 minutes.

Nice touch: Both the tempeh and the veggie "bacon" will work better if you bake at lower temperatures, close to dehydrating them rather than roasting. Try it at 250° for about 30 minutes. Every oven is a bit different and timing will vary.

Buffalo Cauliflower Bites

 30 minutes

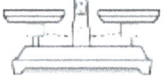

1 cauliflower
¾ cup of whole wheat flour (or cornmeal, chickpea flour, or any other variety of flour)
1 cup plant milk or water
1 teaspoon garlic powder
1 teaspoon salt
1 teaspoon paprika (optional)
1 teaspoon baking powder (optional)
1 Tablespoon flaxseed (optional)
1 cup Buffalo Sauce *(page 40)*

This works wonderfully with cauliflower, but our good friends in Texas have proved anything can be breaded. Try it with onion rings, zucchini, eggplant, broccoli, peppers, mushrooms, sweet potato, string beans, carrot, radishes, etc.

Buffalo Cauliflower Bites

If you are not into hot stuff, these bites will taste great dipped in almost any dressing or sauce in this book: BBQ, Tartar, Thousand Island, Cilantro, Ranch, Curry, etc. Or just Ketchup, Soy Sauce and/or Mustard.

Preheat the oven to 325⁰. Cut cauliflower florets into bite-size pieces. Proper French technique teaches us to cut from the stem: once the stem is cut, pull apart with your hands, and the floret will break apart in a more natural shape than cutting the floret directly with the knife. You may cut the stems into bite sizes and bread them too, and munch on them, as you taste if it is done baking. You can also save the stem for a veggie soup or the Cauliflower Cheese sauce *(page 52)*.

With a whisk (better) or spoon, mix the flour, milk and the seasonings into a batter in a bowl. It has to be just thick enough that it won't run down the florets before you get it in the oven. Toss the cauliflower in the batter and try to get a thick layer to cover the cauliflower bites evenly.

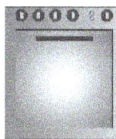 Roast in the oven until nicely tanned, about 15-20 minutes. Meanwhile, rinse the bowl and put the buffalo sauce in it. As soon as you pull the cauliflower out of the oven, toss it with the buffalo sauce and serve, or return to the oven for reheating another few minutes.

Other Ingredients: Some like it real hot, so add more hot sauce and/or chopped chilies or jalapenos.

If you like it a bit crispier, toss the bites in Panko breadcrumbs after covered in batter.

Jackpot: There is a mushroom called Laetiporus, or "Chicken of the Woods". If you ever get your hands on this beauty, it makes a spectacular "chicken finger". It is very dry, so, let it soak in plant milk with a bit of salt and spices for several hours, then use this recipe for breading and roasting.

Unbelievable Potato Salad

 30 minutes  4-6 servings

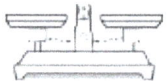 3-4 large Russet or Idaho potatoes, or 8-12 small red or white potatoes
½ to 1 onion
5-10 sprigs parsley
1 cup raw cashews
1 ¼ cup water
3 cloves garlic
2 teaspoons salt
1 teaspoon lemon Juice
¼ cup Dijon mustard

Unbelievable Potato Salad

There are many different styles of potato salad, and this creamy German recipe is my favorite. I am a bit of a purist on this, so I don't add other vegetables; but nothing is preventing you from adding carrots, broccoli, cauliflower, corn, edamame, peppers, peas, chickpeas, etc. My wife believes that capers are absolutely necessary, and I agree they work well. My mom feels the same about raisins; I always thought I was being punished for something, and I probably deserved it.

Cut the potatoes in quarters, then in ¼" slices. The thin slices allow for more surface exposure to the cream. Peeling is optional, I don't peel. Place the cut potatoes immediately in water, either in a bowl or a pot.

Place the pot with cut potatoes and salted water on high heat, bring to boil, then simmer in mid-low for about 10 minutes. Any potato works; chef potatoes (aka Russet) will be a bit more crumbly while red, Yukon, gold and white potatoes will hold their shape better.

While this boils, dice the onion as small as you can, and chop the parsley. Add all other ingredients to a blender and blend well.

Mix everything in a bowl and serve chilled. Warm is not too bad either.

Tip: This is one of those recipes that will taste better the next day(s), once the potatoes soak in the flavor from the cream and seasonings.

You may cut the cashew cream in half, and use Mayo *(page 22)* as well. You may also reduce the amount of cashews and use a piece of tofu or white beans instead.

Other ingredients: you may use a can of coconut milk instead of the cashews and water. It will add a little bit of coconut flavor, which I personally don't mind.

Trick: If you find the salad a bit too dry in the fridge after a couple days, and you are out of mayo or cream, just toss it with a bit of plant milk or water to rehydrate.

Latkes

 30 minutes   4-6 servings

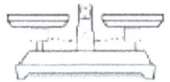
3 large potatoes
½ onion
2 cloves garlic
¼ cup whole wheat flour (or garbanzo, potato or corn starch)
1 teaspoon salt
1 teaspoon baking powder (optional)
1 teaspoon nutrition yeast (optional)
1 tablespoon flaxseed (optional)

At least a dozen European and Middle Eastern countries claim Latkes as a part of their traditional cuisine. It became even more popular around the world as Hanukkah evolved to a major holiday during the XX century. There are many variations to the recipe, and it is traditionally fried. We are offering a baked alternative.

Latkes with Tartar Dressing

Preheat the oven to 325⁰ or a pan on high. If using the oven, a non-stick or parchment sheet will help, or mildly coat the tray with oil.

Shred the potatoes, small-dice the onion and mince the garlic into a bowl. Toss with the flour, seasoning and other ingredients. Scoop heaping tablespoons onto the baking sheet and press them into circles ~2-3" wide. Bake until nicely golden, about 20 minutes. It will release easier when it chills a bit. For stove top, roast in a pan for about 3-5 minutes on each side.

Serve with our Savory Cashew Cream *(page 32),* **Zesty Tahini** *(page 21),* or one of the many sauces and dressings in this book.

Roasted Broccoli

 30 minutes

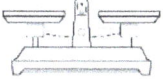
1 head of broccoli
2 Tablespoons mayo or cashew cream
1 teaspoon Easy Veggies Seasoning (or salt + garlic powder)
1 Tablespoon Dijon Mustard
1 Tablespoon Nutritional Yeast

Sometimes I munch on raw broccoli; but it really tastes great roasted. Same is true with cauliflower, which you can roast this way too. This is a minimal effort side or snack, for any time of the day.

Roasted Broccoli with Curry Mayo

Preheat the oven to 325°. Break the florets from the larger stem, then break them down to bite size pieces. You may roast the stems too, or save it to use for a soup *(page 142),* or chop them small for Veggies with Curry *(page 82)* or a Couscous *(page 76).* In a large bowl, toss the broccoli florets in ~2 tablespoons of cashew cream, mayo or zesty tahini; or even 2 tablespoons of plant milk with a teaspoon of Dijon and tablespoon of flour. We don't need a lot of liquid, nor are we breading. The goal is to help the seasoning to attach to the broccoli. Then toss it a bit more, with the Easy Veggies seasoning, your preferred seasoning mix, or just lemon pepper or salt and garlic powder.

Bake until you see tanning on the florets, around 12 minutes. Start checking at 10 minutes, so they don't burn.

Salsa

⏱ 10 minutes

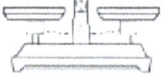

1 tomato
½ onion
½ pepper
¼ cucumber or a rib of celery
1-2 cloves garlic
3 sprigs cilantro
1 Tablespoon lemon juice
1 teaspoon hot sauce
½ to 1 teaspoon salt

Salsa and Guacamole

There is absolutely no need to buy salsa at the supermarket; make it fresh.

Dice the vegetables as small as you can, and gently toss in a bowl with the seasoning.

Other Ingredients: There are many possible ingredients and variations. Replace any of the ingredients with, or add corn, beans, black-eyed peas, avocado, pineapple, mango, edamame or peas.

Guacamole

Set aside half of the Salsa recipe and add 2 avocados, diced small, for an excellent Guacamole. Add a bit more salt if you prefer.

Stuffed Banana Peppers

 25 minutes

 **8 Banana or Cubanelle Peppers**
2 cups Basic Rice *(page 55)*
1 cup Basic or Savory Cashew Cream *(page 32)*
½ to 1 pound mushrooms or random veggies
1 cup Hollandaise *(page 28)*

Stuffed Banana Peppers with Mushroom and Peppers Risotto

Not so funny story: One of my first tasks in the restaurant world was to prep some 200 stuffed banana peppers. To make some stupid macho point, I refused to wear gloves. My fingers burned for a week.

 Preheat the oven to 350℉.

Open a slit on one side of the banana peppers lengthwise from the stem to the other edge, then cut it in a cross shape at the stem, so you can spread the pepper open without dismantling it.

Roast the mushrooms or random veggies, and then mix with the rice and cashew cream, into a soft but not too runny mix. Stuff the peppers with as much filling as you can fit. Use a toothpick, if you like, to close it. Place the peppers on a tray and bake until nicely browned, about 15 minutes. The roasting of the peppers will bring out the sweetness of the pepper and reduce the spice heat. It is hard to predict how spicy the peppers are, but they tend to get less spicy as they ripen. Cubanelle peppers tend to be hardly spicy at all.

Pour the Hollandaise sauce over the peppers and serve hot.

Other Ingredients: You may use the leftovers of a Risotto *(page 71)* to stuff the peppers. You may use regular peppers, instead of banana peppers, red ones will be tastier than green. If you are stuffing tomatoes, add some oats to the stuffing and make it dry, so it absorbs some of the tomato's moisture.

You may use various veggies in addition to or instead of mushrooms like you'd do with risotto: asparagus, red peppers, corn, palm hearts, artichokes, peas, etc.

You may use any other sauce from this book over the peppers, to garnish and complement the flavor.

Nice Touch: Add capers or chopped olives to the sauce.

Roasted Eggplant

 30 minutes

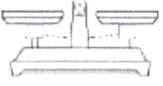

1 large eggplant
¾ cup of whole wheat flour (chickpea flour also works great),
½ cup plant milk or water
1 teaspoon garlic powder
1 teaspoon onion powder
1 teaspoon salt
1 teaspoon baking powder (optional)

1 cup Panko style breadcrumbs
1 cup to 1 pint of tomato sauce

I love eggplant, but it is, perhaps, the most challenging vegetable to cook. It is horrendous when undercooked and becomes mushy and soggy when overcooked. The roasting time varies from other veggies, but that can be solved by cutting it thinner and smaller than the other vegetables. I find it safest to cook it in a casserole pot, such as cooking in the curry sauce along with potatoes and other veggies. Or you may bread it and roast it in the oven. When breaded, it self-adjusts the moisture, and will still have crispiness, even if you overcook. It's easy to tell when it's done, by the tanning of the breading.

Roasted Eggplant

Preheat the oven to 325°. Mix the flour, milk, and seasoning into a batter in a deep plate. Cut the eggplant in ¼ to ½ inch slices, and pat dry with a paper towel. Dip the slices in the batter, getting a thick layer on each side. Then dip it in the breadcrumbs. Lay the breaded slices on a non-stick tray and bake until nicely tanned, about 20 minutes. Meanwhile, heat the tomato sauce in a pot. After the eggplant is baked, spread the tomato sauce over the slices, and serve.

Tip: Make a bunch of it; it's great for sandwiches the next day(s)!

Easy Chocolate Mousse

 10 minutes

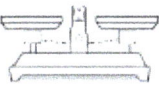
1-3 Tablespoons of unsweetened chocolate/cocoa powder
¼ to ½ cup raw sugar
¼ to ½ teaspoon vanilla extract
0 - ¼ cup plant milk
1 pack silken tofu
¼ teaspoon Kosher salt

This is the easiest possible recipe for a mousse. The type and quality of the cocoa powder determine the result and how much of it you want to use. You probably only need one tablespoon of pure dark cocoa powder.

It is also important to use a high-quality firm/extra firm silken tofu. Regular tofu doesn't have the right texture, and has too much of an after-taste.

If you have extra-firm silken tofu that is truly firm, the type you can hold in your hand, start with adding the chocolate, sugar, salt, plant milk and vanilla to the food processor or blender and run it for about a minute, until the sugar and chocolate dissolve perfectly. Then add the tofu and blend well. If it's a softer tofu, add all but the milk to the blender, at the same time. The blender will blend it better than a processor, but it will be harder to scoop it out. If it is too thick to blend well, add a bit more plant milk.

Other ingredients: For a richer mousse, add ½ cup of raw cashews to the blender, at the beginning. You may use a can of coconut milk instead of the tofu, with ¼ cup of cornstarch. If the canned coconut milk is not very thick, you may need to bring it to boil. It will add a little bit of coconut flavor, which I personally don't mind.
There are many flavors you may add to the mousse: orange peels, fruit jam, liqueur, or any nut, either when blending or in the cup.

Shiish! Too runny: you may add cashews, nuts, tahini or a teaspoon of cornstarch to the blender. It will get a bit thicker when chilled.

Those who take chocolate very seriously will prefer to melt solid chocolate in bain marie, instead of using powder. If you love chocolate, I very strongly recommend the book "Vegan Chocolate", by my incredibly talented friend, Fran Costigan. An excellent mousse is just one of many of her spectacular recipes.

Soups

Cream of Kale - Creamy Vegetable Soup

 25 minutes   4-6 servings

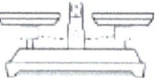
- 1 large onion
- 1 potato
- 1 pound kale (or any of your favorite veggies)
- 2 cloves garlic
- 1 cup raw cashews
- ½ Tablespoon salt
- 1 quart water

Cream of Kale

Pre-heat a pan on high, or the oven to 350℉. Sautee or roast the onion and potato until it starts to brown. Drizzle water into the pan if it begins to stick. Add the kale and garlic and cook/roast for another 5-10 minutes.

Add the veggies, water, and all other ingredients to the blender and blend without mercy, until it's smooth enough that you wouldn't need to strain.

Reheat, to serve hot.

This is what we call a "ratio recipe": you may use it replacing the kale for one pound of pretty much any other main vegetable, keeping the same remaining ingredients

Other ingredient options:
Some ideas are:

- broccoli, celery, spinach, asparagus, pepper, using the same other ingredients in the recipe
- roasted tomato, adding 2 carrots
- carrots, adding a tablespoon of ginger powder, pinch of nutmeg
- butternut squash or pumpkin, adding ¼ teaspoon cinnamon, a pinch of nutmeg

Feel encouraged to add your preferred seasoning and herbs to the soup: soy sauce, hot sauce, spice mixes, chopped parsley, green onions or dill. Add seasoning in small increments and taste to see if it's working.

Leek & Potato

 35 minutes   4-6 servings

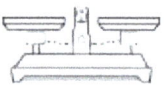
1 ½ pounds potato
8 oz onion
2 cloves garlic
1 small leek
½ to 1 cup raw cashews
1 quart water or plant milk
1 teaspoon salt
1 teaspoon sugar
1 teaspoon Miso (optional)

Preheat the oven to 350⁰ or a pan on mid-high. Dice the potatoes and onions in about ¼ inch and roast until lightly browned, about 10 minutes. Chop the leek and mince the garlic and roast them separately for about 5 minutes; don't let it burn.

Use about ½ of the potatoes and onions to blend with the cashews, water, and seasoning. Blend without mercy until smooth.

Pour blended soup into a pot with the remaining potatoes, onions, leek, and garlic and bring it to boil. Check if the potato is fully cooked and serve.

Other Ingredients: Edamame, carrot and red pepper will make the soup nicely colorful.

Nice Touch: Garnish with green onions and Tempeh Bacon *(page 129)*.

Ajiaco

For a homesick Colombian, add to the Leak and Potato 8oz of roasted corn, 1 teaspoon turmeric, 5 sprigs of cilantro and 1 Tablespoon of dried guasca, a Colombian herb that can be found online or at some Latin stores. Garnish with capers and cilantro and serve with fresh avocado. A proud Colombian will say it's not the same without the local Criolla potato, but they are just being picky. If you can't find guasca, however, it won't taste at all like Ajiaco.

Creamy Gazpacho

 20 minutes   4 servings

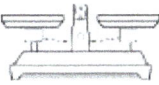
2 cucumbers
1 tomato
1 clove garlic
½ pepper
1 tablespoon lemon juice
1 leaf kale
¼ cup cashews
1 teaspoon salt
1 Tablespoon Dijon mustard
1 teaspoon hot sauce
1 pint water

Add all the veggies and ingredients to the blender and blend lightly for a rustic finish or blend without mercy for a very smooth texture. Serve chilled in a bowl, garnished with diced cucumber, pepper and/or tomatoes. You can also serve in a glass as a savory smoothie.

Gazpacho

Other Ingredients: You may add other mild veggies you may have sitting in the fridge. I don't recommend raw onions. They are too strong tasting.

Tip: If you would like a redder tomato color, you may add a bit of tomato paste or roasted, dried or canned tomatoes (as in the picture). You won't get a solid red color from fresh tomatoes. The color will look more solid ½ hour after the blending, as the foaming settles.

Chili

 3 hours (20 minutes hands on)  4 servings

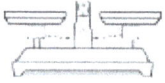
1 cup black bean (dry)
1 cup white bean (dry)
1 cup red Kidney bean (dry)
1 cup pinto bean (dry)
1 teaspoon garlic powder
1 Tablespoon cumin
½ Tablespoon coriander
1 Tablespoon oregano (mix of rosemary/thyme also works)
1 Tablespoon salt
¼ to ½ cup raw sugar
3 cloves garlic cloves
1 Tablespoon Braggs Aminos
1 cup tomato sauce (or ketchup)
1 Tablespoon hot sauce
1 onion
1 tomato
1 carrot
2 ribs of celery
5 sprigs cilantro

Chili is another great way to have your legumes. You can use a variety of beans; I like to combine at least 3 types of beans.

Chili, shortcut style, with summer zucchini and squash

The Easiest Plant-Based Recipe Book Ever. Everyday Vegan Cooking.

 Soak beans overnight, or for at least one hour in water seasoned with the garlic powder. Drain, rinse and add the beans to a pot with all the seasonings and the minced garlic. Either add all the other veggies diced, or roast them separately and add them at the end. Add water until it covers the beans by one inch. Bring to boil, reduce temperature and simmer for 1.5 to 4 hours stirring occasionally. The longer it cooks, the thicker and richer it will be. Take a peek every half hour and see if it needs more water. Chop the cilantro and add it right before serving.

Slow cooker: if you have a slow cooker, add all ingredients except the cilantro and let it cook for some 6-8 hours.

Shortcut: canned beans. Use 4-6 cans of various beans and rinse them well. Instead of cooking the soup, blend ~1/3 of the beans in 1 quart of water, roast the veggies and mix it all together in a pot. Bring to simmer. It will not have the same taste, texture, and color, but it's a shortcut.

Other Ingredients: Add shredded seitan, tofu, tempeh or ground texturized vegetable protein. It also works to add barley, corn, bulgur or quinoa.

Shiish: Too runny. Blend one or two ladles of the beans and return to the pot, bringing it to boil.

Borscht

 35 minutes   4-6 servings

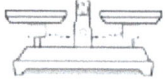

½ onion
1 red pepper
1 potato
1 tomato
¼ to ½ red cabbage (regular cabbage is ok too)
2 ribs of celery (kale stems, cauliflower or broccoli trimmings are fine too)
1 pound beets
1 carrot
2 mushrooms
3 sprigs fresh cilantro
1 teaspoon dried dill
1 ½ quarts water
1 teaspoon lemon juice
1 teaspoon paprika
¼ teaspoon cayenne
1 Tablespoon salt
1 Tablespoon soy sauce

Borscht, fully blended with Cashew Cream

Borscht can be a blended or chunky soup. I prefer mostly blended. That decision will drive how you cut the veggies: rough cuts for blending, nice dicing or shredding for chunky. You may do a combination of both, by setting aside veggies that you will use for garnishing after blending, like about half of the diced or shredded carrots and beets.

If your family comes from Germany, Russia, Ukraine, Poland, Hungary or around that region, there is a strong possibility someone related to you has a secret family recipe for the absolute best borsch ever. Honor your family's tradition and use it! Just skip the meat and replace the beef stock with a bit of soy sauce.

Preheat the oven to 350⁰ or a large pot on medium-high. Roast all the veggies to a nice brown. Either pour water into the pot and mix with the vegetables and seasoning or blend all or some of the roasted veggies with some of the water before adding it all to the pot.

Serve hot or cold with a generous drizzle of the Savory Cashew Cream *(page 32)*.

Shortcut: you may use canned beets. The color and flavor will not be the same because a lot is lost in the brine.

Other ingredients: Golden beets will work fine, just with a different color. You don't need to use all the veggies listed in the recipe, and you may use other vegetables in varying amounts. The only critical ingredient is beet.

Coconut Mushroom Soup

 30 minutes   4-6 servings

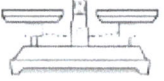
2 onions
1 green pepper
1 red pepper
2 tomatoes
2 cloves garlic
10+ mushrooms
1 pint water
1 teaspoon lemon juice
2 teaspoons salt
1 Tablespoon raw sugar or maple syrup
1 teaspoon paprika
1 teaspoon hot sauce
1 quart coconut Milk
~5 sprigs cilantro

There's a dish in the Northeast of Brazil called Moqueca; it is typically made with seafood and resembles Thai cuisine. This is a variation that can be served as a soup or over rice or couscous.

Preheat the oven to 350⁰, or a pan on high. Slice mushrooms very thin. If there are Portobello stems, roast the clean portion of the stems (discard the portion with dirt) separately to blend, or dice them very small. Dice all other veggies. Don't be shy with the mushrooms, if you have more, use more.

Roast all vegetables in the oven or in a pot stirring occasionally, until they are nicely browned.

Scoop a cup, not all, of the veggies and all the roasted mushroom stems into the blender and blend with all the seasoning and water. Blend the cilantro at the end at low speed, not to pulverize it.

Return the blended liquid to a pot; mix with the veggies and coconut milk. Bring to a boil,  and simmer for a few minutes. The thickness will depend on the coconut milk you used. For this soup, I prefer the canned Thai type of coconut milk, because it has a delicious and bolder flavor. It may need some additional diluting with a bit more water or plant milk.

Coconut Mushroom Soup

Veggie Miso Soup

 25 minutes   4-6 servings

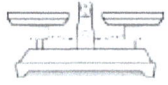

1 onion
~5 mushrooms
1 carrot
3 pints water
1 rib celery
4 Tablespoons miso
3 Tablespoon soy sauce
1 teaspoon lemon juice
1 sheet nori
4 oz tofu
A drizzle of hot sauce or a pinch of black pepper

Veggie Miso Soup

This is one of the few clear soups that I like. I like to spice it up with a lively hot sauce, wasabi or minced fresh chili peppers.

Heat up a large pot. Slice the mushrooms and dice the onions, carrot, and celery. You may add other vegetables, like potato, peppers, broccoli or cauliflower. Roast the veggies to lightly brown and add all other ingredients.

Bring to boil and let it simmer for 5 to 15 minutes.

Make it creamy: If you prefer creamy soups, blend all or some of the soup with a ¼ cup of raw cashews.

Shiish: It tastes a bit bland: Just add more soy sauce or miso, which will also increase the sodium level. You may stir in a bit of hot sauce, wasabi or ginger.

Nice touch: You may garnish with roughly chopped fresh green onions. Baked tofu will taste better than tofu just out of the package.

Pho, Udon, Ramen, and other Asian noodles

Professional chefs tend to cook quick and simple recipes at home. Ramen is one favorite of several chefs I know, for being super-quick.

While I can see the appeal to practicality, I suggest that you stay away from the little packs of Ramen bricks. That stuff is terrible. It's packed with fat, because it's fried, has very little nutritional value, and contain nasty preservatives like Tertiary-butyl hydroquinone (TBHQ). People have found packs in their homes that are over 10 years old and still look "good". If bacteria and fungi have a hard time eating it, we should take the hint that it's probably not great for human consumption and digestion either. Look for brown rice Pho noodles, buckwheat or whole wheat Soba or Udon noodles, or, really, any variety of noodles you like, preferably from whole grains. Unless you are cooking for your picky mother-in-law that will know the difference and will be culturally offended, just use the one you like best.

The Vegies Miso Soup *(page 152)* recipe is a great foundation for an Asian noodle soup, like the popular Vietnamese Pho, Japanese Udon and Ramen or a variety of oriental noodles. The common ground of these soups is that they all require making a broth, and usually use a few simple vegetables. There are, of course, various particular ingredients and broth making techniques that make each of these soups regionally unique; and it's exciting and delicious to explore all the possibilities arising from such a basic concept. Major differences in the authentic recipes will be the type of noodle, the broth seasoning, herbs and spices, and the vegetables used for cooking and garnishg the soup.

For the purpose of this book, we will keep it simple using basic and easy-to-find ingredients.

Ramen and Udon

 35 minutes   2-4 servings

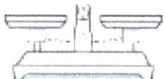

1 Recipe Miso Soup *(page 152)*
12 oz to 1 pound of Ramen or Udon noodles
¼ Red Pepper
1 Cup Edamame
1 Carrot
5 Mushrooms
1 head Broccoli
1 bunch of green onions (for garnishing)

Udon Noodles

In one pot, start boiling water with a teaspoon of salt, to cook the noodles. Follow the cooking instructions on the noodles pack.

Meanwhile, start the Miso Soup recipe in another pot, using the veggies in the Miso recipe or any vegetables you like; carrots, onions, and mushroom are an easy combination. Feel free to use anything you have, like peas, broccoli, cauliflower, etc. Save the green onions for garnishing. Bamboo shoots are a nice touch if you found them where you bought the noodles. Strain the cooked noodles, and check if the veggies in the Miso broth are cooked, ~ 8 minutes. Easier to serve the strained noodles to a bowl and then top it with the broth. Garnish with green onions.

Tofu Pho

 30 minutes   2-4 servings

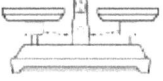

1 recipe Miso Soup *(page 152)*
12 oz to 1 pound of brown rice Pho noodles
1 carrot, sliced very thin or shredded
2 cups of shredded cabbage
1 pack of tofu
1 thick slice of ginger or ¼ teaspoon of ginger powder

In one pot, start boiling water with a teaspoon of salt, to cook the noodles. Follow the cooking instructions on the noodles pack.

Meanwhile, if you didn't marinate and bake tofu per the recipe *(page 125)*, cut the tofu in ½" cubes, toss in a bowl with 2 tablespoons of soy sauce and bake in the oven for ~10-15 minutes.

Start the Miso Soup recipe in another pot *(page 152)*, adding ginger, and using the veggies in the Miso recipe or any veggies you like; cauliflower, peas, and peppers are an easy combination. Feel free to use anything you have, like broccoli, mushrooms, etc. Save the carrots and cabbage for garnishing.

Strain the cooked noodles, and check if the veggies in the Miso broth are cooked, ~ 8 minutes. It's easier to serve the strained noodles to a bowl and then top it with the broth. Garnish with shredded carrots and cabbage.

Thai Coconut Noodles

 30 minutes  2-4 servings

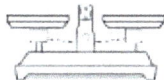

1 recipe Miso Soup *(152)*, **replacing 1 pint of water with 1 can of coconut milk.**
12 oz to 1 pound of brown rice noodles
1 thick slice of ginger or ¼ teaspoon of ginger powder
1-2 teaspoons curry powder
½ teaspoon paprika
1-2 teaspoons sugar
1 teaspoon lemon juice
¼ bunch basil and/or cilantro
Adding Lemon grass to the broth is a nice touch

Thai Coconut Noodles

In one pot, start boiling water with a teaspoon of salt, to cook the noodles. Follow the cooking instructions on the noodles pack.

Meanwhile, start the Miso Soup recipe in another pot, using the veggies in the Miso recipe or any veggies you like; carrots, broccoli, onions, and mushroom are an easy combination. Remember to replace one pint of water with a can of coconut milk. Add the curry, paprika, sugar and lemon juice. Save the basil and/or cilantro for garnishing. Strain the cooked noodles, check if the veggies in the Miso broth are cooked, ~ 8 minutes, and combine the noodles with the broth. Serve and garnish with the basil and/or cilantro.

Breakfast

Arepas *(Corn Cakes)* – Traditional

 30 minutes 4-6 servings

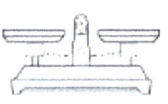
2 cups arepa flour (Masarepa/precooked cornmeal)
2 ½ to 3 cups of water
1-2 teaspoon salt

Arepas are expected on any breakfast table in Colombia and Venezuela. In Colombia they are traditionally eaten plain, with a light spread; in Venezuela, they are often filled and stuffed with anything they can get their hands on, sandwich style.

Arepas are a corn patty, cousin of polenta or tamales. It requires a special flour made of precooked cornmeal, which is easy to find in supermarkets across America. Using polenta or cornmeal is an alternative, but will render something of a different consistency.

Warm up the salted water, but not to boil; just hot enough that your hands will still stand the heat when kneading. Pour it over the flour in a bowl, start mixing with a spatula and eventually finish with your hands. Adjust the moisture. The dough has to be firm enough to keep the shape of a ball, but not too dry. Preheat a pan on high, and then reduce down to medium-high. Or preheat the oven to 325⃣.

Make balls slightly smaller than a golf ball, then, pressing inside your hands, flatten them to a circle and place directly on the pan or on a baking sheet. Cook for about 5 minutes on each side, or bake for ~10-12 minutes in the oven.

Arepas (Corn Cakes) - How I like it

 30 minutes   4-6 servings

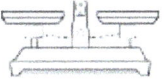
- 2 cups arepa flour (Masarepa/precooked cornmeal)
- 3 cups of water
- 2 Tablespoons flaxseed
- 1 Tablespoon nutritional yeast
- 1 Tablespoon baking powder
- ¼ teaspoon garlic powder
- 1-2 teaspoons salt

Arepas – How I like it, roasted on a pan

Some changes that add a bit of flavor and crust to the traditional recipe.

Warm the salted water, but not to boil; just hot enough that your hands will still stand the heat when kneading. Mix the dry ingredients in a large bowl, and then pour the water in. Start mixing with a spatula and eventually finish with your hands. Adjust the moisture: the dough has to be firm enough to keep the shape of a ball, but not too dry. Preheat a pan on high, and then reduce down to medium-high. Or preheat the oven to 325°.

Make balls slightly bigger than a golf ball, then, pressing inside your hands, flatten them to a circle and place directly on the pan or on a baking sheet. Cook for about 5 minutes on each side or bake for ~10-12 minutes in the oven.

Tofu Scramble

 30 minutes   4 servings

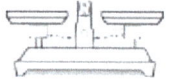
1 onion
2 cloves garlic
1 pack of extra firm tofu (12-16oz, regular or silken)
½ pepper
4 mushrooms
1 handful of spinach
¼ teaspoon turmeric (optional)
1 teaspoon salt

Tofu Scramble and whole-wheat wrap

Tofu scramble is quick-and-easy. However, if you have time, like many other tofu recipes, this works best if you cook slowly at a mid-low temperature. It allows for the tofu to dehydrate and form a nicer texture.

Preheat a pan to medium, or the oven at 300°. The pan is fine, but the oven is more efficient for larger batches, often forms a better texture and you don't need to keep stirring it.

Dice the onions and pepper, mince the garlic and slice the mushrooms. Add all veggies to a pot and roast them slightly before adding the tofu, so to remove some of the moist. Crumble the tofu with your hands into the pan, spread the seasoning, toss and mix well. Works better to cook slowly, at medium, stirring occasionally and gently not to mash the crumbles. If you stir and flip too often, you won't allow a nice roasting crust to form on the tofu. You may speed it up, by cranking up to mid-high, stirring a bit more frequently. About 15 minutes.

If using the oven, mix the hand crumbled tofu with the veggies and seasoning and, lay it on a baking sheet or pan and roast at 300-325°. It is ready when the tofu starts to brown, forming a nice crust, about 15-20 minutes.

Regular or silken tofu is a matter of personal preference for texture.

Nice Touch: *top it with Hollandaise (page 28).*

Easy Quiche

 20 min prep, 30 min baking, 15 min setting  4 servings

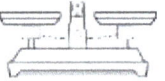
1 pack of tofu
3-5 cloves of garlic
1 teaspoon salt
¼ to ½ cup of plant milk (depends on the tofu)
1 teaspoon Dijon mustard (optional)
1 Tablespoon cornstarch (optional)
1 Tablespoon nutritional yeast (optional)
2 Tablespoons of flaxseed meal (optional)
½ teaspoon turmeric (optional)
½ large onion
½ pepper
2 mushrooms
1 handful of spinach or kale
1 cup oats

This is perhaps the easiest recipe for a plant-based quiche. The downside is that it has to chill entirely after baking, for it to set well. I like to make it the day before brunch and reheat in the oven.

You can make this French staple in a large pie mold, or, as I prefer, in smaller silicon muffin molds or deep burger molds.

Easy Quiche with Hollandaise

Regular or silken tofu is a matter of personal preference for texture. Use silken tofu for a smoother texture.

Preheat the oven to 300-315℉. Lower oven temperatures with longer baking allow the tofu to lose moisture and set better. If you are using good quality silicone or non-stick molds, you should be fine. If your molds are not non-stick or have seen better days, you may brush with a small amount of oil.

Slice or dice the veggies, larger for a pie-sized quiche or smaller if you are using muffing/burger sizes. Season and toss the veggies with a bit of salt and garlic powder or the Easy Veggies Seasoning *(page 19)* and distribute them in the mold(s), about 1/3 of the way up. Don't forcibly pack it tight; you want them to be permeated by the batter.

Blend all the non-veggie ingredients (except the oats) to a batter, as thick as possible. If it is so thick that it won't blend, add a bit more plant milk. Pour the batter over the veggies in the mold, filling it to ~3/4 of the way up. Do not rinse the blender yet; we will use what's left in there for our "crust". Sprinkle a ¼" layer of oats over the batter, then, use a little plant milk or water to release what's left of the batter in the blender, then pour enough of that liquid onto the oats to fully moisten them.

Bake for 30 minutes for smaller molds, 40 minutes for pie molds, at 300-315℉, or pull it out a few minutes short if it starts to burn.

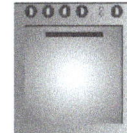

It will be easier to remove the quiche from the mold(s) after it chills completely and sets.

Other Fillings: Use your favorite veggies, like asparagus, artichoke, kale, eggplant, Portobello, broccoli, zucchini, cauliflower, corn, peas, etc.

Or use onion, corn, beans, peppers, and cilantro for a Mexican style (topped with a tomato sauce seasoned with cilantro).

Nice Touch: serve the quiche with Hollandaise *(page 28)* and chopped green onions.

Spanish Tortilla

 20 min prep, 40 min baking, 30 min setting  4 servings

1 pack of tofu
3-5 cloves of garlic
1 teaspoon salt
¼ to ½ cup of plant milk (depends on the tofu)
1 teaspoon Dijon mustard (optional)
1 Tablespoon cornstarch (optional)
1 Tablespoon nutritional yeast (optional)
2 Tablespoons of flaxseed meal (optional)
½ teaspoon turmeric (optional)
1 large potato
½ large onion
½ pepper
2 mushrooms

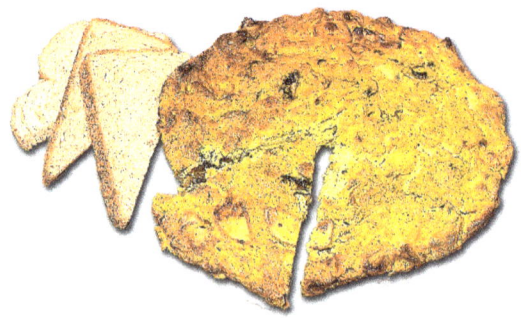

Spanish Tortilla

For the Spanish, tortilla is breakfast, bar food or anytime snack. We can make it plant-based! The downside is that it has to bake at low heat and has to chill entirely after baking, for it to set well. I like to make it the day before brunch and reheat in the oven.

Dice the potato, or cut in in ½, lengthwise, and slice half-moons, then boil or roast it with the other veggies, while you blend the batter.

Make the batter as thick a batter as possible. If it is so thick that it won't blend, add a bit more plant milk. You may also cook ~1 cup of whole-wheat pasta instead of potato.

Gently fold the veggies, cooked potato or pasta into the batter, then pour the batter to a pie or baking mold (s) and bake for ~40 minutes at 300-315°. It will be easier to remove from the mold(s) after it chills completely and sets.

Other ingredients: traditional Spanish Tortillas use potatoes, garlic, and onions only. Those of us who are always on the lookout for opportunities to diversify our veggies, feel an urge to add stuff. Spinach, peppers, kale, peas are all good choices. I'd stay away from tomatoes or other very moist vegetables because our goal is to remove moisture from the tofu as we bake.

Grits

 30 minutes   4-6 servings

1 cup of grits
½ cup quinoa (optional)
2 cups of water
2 ½ cups of plant milk
1 teaspoon salt
1 teaspoon garlic powder
1 onion
1-2 peppers
6 mushrooms
3-5 kale leaves or a handful of spinach

½ cup of water
½ cup of cashews
2 garlic cloves
½ teaspoon salt
½ teaspoon Dijon mustard

Here in Pennsylvania, grits are not a traditional breakfast item. So, a man goes to Georgia and carelessly utters he doesn't really see much in grits. What words just passed the barrier of his teeth! Disappointed desperation will turn into determined conviction: they won't let you leave until you learn to adore the thing. Soon enough, you see the beauty and the possibilities.

Grits, with roasted veggies and Savory Cashew Cream

Mix the first portion of the recipe: grits, water, milk, and seasoning, in a medium pot and bring to simmer, stirring occasionally to keep the bottom from burning. While it cooks, about 20 minutes, slice, dice, and roast the veggies. Feel free to use any vegetables you like or have in the fridge, freezer or pantry.

While the grits cook and the veggies roast, blend the 3rd portion of the recipe, which is the cashew cream. Once the grits cook to a nice creamy consistency, pour them onto bowls or plates, top with the vegetables and cashew cream and serve.

Polenta and grits are essentially the same thing but made from different types of corn, with slightly different processing. Typically, polenta is made from a yellower corn and ground coarsely, and grits are made from whiter corn. If all you have is polenta, you may use it for grits, even if the purists scream in horror. If you bought instant grits, follow the instructions on the pack for the amount of liquid and cooking time.

I am not sure if it is part of the tradition, but I've noticed people eating hot sauce with a little bit of grits added to it.

You may have it sweet too; just don't show it to my friends in Atlanta. In that case, you won't need the veggies or the cashew cream. Reduce the salt, eliminate the garlic, and add 2 tablespoons of raw brown sugar, ½ teaspoon of cinnamon and a pinch of nutmeg. Serve with fruit, fruit preserves, raisins and/or a little splash of maple syrup.

Potato Scramble

 25 minutes   4 servings

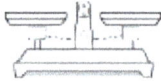 **3-4 large potatoes**
1 large onion
1 tomato
½ teaspoon turmeric (optional)
1 teaspoon salt
1 teaspoon hot sauce
1 Tablespoon Dijon (or your favorite) mustard

Potato Scramble

Preheat a pan at medium-high, or the oven at 350℉.

Dice the onions and tomato, and add to a bowl with all the seasonings. Rinse and scrub the potatoes (peeling is optional, I don't). Dice and toss them in the bowl with all other ingredients and a drizzle of water, just enough to help the salt and turmeric to dissolve and mix with the potatoes.

Pour all ingredients into the pan or a tray for the oven. Roast in the pan until the potatoes are fully cooked or in the oven until browned. About 15 minutes.

Other ingredients: Add your favorite seasoning, like lemon-pepper or Old Bay.

Add other veggies like peppers, squash or mushrooms.

Top or toss with a ½ cup of Savory cashew cream *(page 32)*, Hollandaise *(page 28)* or Zesty Tahini *(page 21)* just before serving.

Everyday Cereal

 20 minutes 4-6 servings

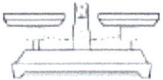
2 cups water
2 cups plant milk
1 cup whole grains hot cereal or oats
½ cup raisins
¼ teaspoon salt
1-2 Tablespoons sugar
¼ teaspoon cinnamon
¼ teaspoon vanilla extract
pinch of nutmeg

This is a lot better and more satisfying than cornflakes with cold milk.

Add the water and milk to a pot and bring to boil. Then lower the heat, add the cereal and seasoning and simmer, stirring occasionally not to burn the bottom. About 10-15 minutes, until it reaches the consistency you like. Add more plant milk if needed.

Other Ingredients: Works well with oats.

You may use any dry or fresh fruits in any amount, either for cooking or garnishing.

Nice Touch: Garnish with chopped nuts and/or fruits, a splash of plant milk and a drizzle of maple syrup.

Hot cereal garnished with raisins, apple, and a splash of maple syrup

Pancakes

 20 minutes 4 servings

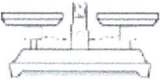
2 cups whole wheat flour
2 Tablespoons baking powder
¼ teaspoon salt
3 Tablespoons raw brown sugar
Pinch cinnamon (optional)
Pinch nutmeg (optional)
1 cup plant milk
1 cup Cashew Cream *(page 30)*
1 teaspoon vanilla extract (optional)
1 Tablespoon flaxseed meal (optional)

Mix the dry ingredients first, and then add the liquids. Mix gently with a whisk or a spatula. We are looking for a thick batter, neither a dough nor a runny liquid; adjust by adding more plant milk or flour.

Pre-heat a large non-stick pan on medium. Gently pour the batter with a 4oz ladle or measuring cup. Let it cook until you see that it looks bubbly in the center and cooked around the edges, about 3 minutes. Flip it with a flipping spatula and let it cook for another 2-3 minutes.

It will work on waffle irons; may require you to spray it with oil.

Serve with fruit, fruit spread or go crazy and pour on a bit of maple syrup.

How to mess it up: if you over-mix you will overwork the gluten in the flour, and the pancakes will become hard. If that happens, it will help to let the batter sit for some 20 minutes before cooking.

Nice Touch: serious bakers will tell you that there is no such thing as "all-purpose flour", that high-gluten Bread Flour is for bread, and Pastry Flour is more adequate for pancakes and cakes. If you find whole-wheat pastry flour in your supermarket, your pancakes will be fluffier.

Other ingredients: We are using cashew cream for a richer batter. You may use plant milk only or canned coconut milk.

Pancakes - Gluten Free

 30 minutes 4 servings

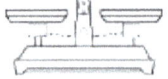
2 cups garbanzo (chickpea) flour
2 Tablespoons baking powder
¼ teaspoon salt
3 Tablespoons raw brown sugar
Pinch cinnamon (optional)
Pinch nutmeg (optional)
1 cup plant milk
1 cup **Cashew Cream** *(page 30)*
1 banana or 1 cup of applesauce (optional)
1 teaspoon vanilla extract (optional)
1 Tablespoon flaxseed meal (optional)

Pancakes – Gluten Free

Mix everything in a blender or food processor. We are looking for a thick batter, but not a dough or a runny liquid; adjust by adding more plant milk or flour.

Pre-heat a large non-stick pan and bring it down to medium-low. Gently pour the batter with a 4oz ladle or measuring cup. Let it cook until you see that it looks bubbly in the center and cooked around the edges, about 3-5 minutes. Flip it with a flipping spatula and let it cook for another 3 minutes.

This will work on waffle irons; may require you to spray it with oil.

Serve with fruit, fruit spread or go crazy and pour on a bit of maple syrup.

How to mess it up: Garbanzo flour is great for gluten-free baking, nice and fluffy, but it has a very noticeable and unpleasant flavor when uncooked. It is crucial that you cook it well, in mid-low, so that the outside doesn't burn before the inside is cooked. If you still dislike the taste of the garbanzo flour, replace half of the garbanzo flour with a fine cornmeal, rice flour or another of the many gluten-free baking flours.

Other ingredients: We are using cashew cream for a richer batter. You may use plant milk only or canned coconut milk.

Sample Meal Plan

Sunday	**Lunch:** Tofu Meatballs *126* and Mashed Potatoes *58*. Choose a sauce, Tomato *46,* Savory Cashew Cream *32* or Mushroom Gravy *44* work great. Make a double batch of mashed potatoes for Tuesday's Shepherd's pie *86*. Make a larger batch of the meatballs and use leftovers for Monday's Sandwich and Lentils. **Dinner:** Salad *100*. Choose a dressing, we have suggestions in the Salads section. **Prep:** Soak 3-4 cups of lentils.
Monday	**Lunch:** Meatball sandwich *114*. **Dinner:** Lentils *62* (you may finish off the leftover meatballs) and Rice *55* (make a double batch of rice and use the leftovers for Wednesday's Curry, and Thursday's fried rice).
Tuesday	**Lunch:** Quinoa Tabbouleh *103*. **Dinner:** Shepherd's Pie *86,* with the leftover Lentils and Mashed Potatoes. (Roast a lot of veggies for the next 3 days). **Prep:** Marinate one or two packs of Tofu *125*.
Wednesday	**Lunch:** Easy Banh Mi *117*, baking the marinated tofu. **Dinner:** Veggies Curry *82* and Rice *55*. Use some of the leftover tofu, if you like.
Thursday	**Lunch:** Last Minute Bowl *78*. Use some of the leftover tofu, if you like. **Dinner:** Fried Rice *66*, use leftover roasted veggies and baked tofu. Choose a sauce, like Zesty Tahini *21,* Curry *50* or Spicy Peanut *42.*
Friday	**Lunch:** Roasted Veggies Tacos *80*, to kill the leftover roasted veggies. Choose a sauce or dressing, I like Cilantro *26*. **Dinner:** Tofu Scramble *160* wrap; and save leftovers for Saturday's breakfast.
Saturday	**Lunch:** Pasta Primavera *88*. Choose a sauce; Tomato *46,* Savory Cashew Cream *32* or Mushroom Gravy *44* work great. **Dinner:** Sushi *68 - 69*.

Sunday	**Lunch:** Black Beans *60* and Rice *55*. **Dinner:** Stuffed Banana Peppers *134* (use rice leftovers from lunch). Choose a sauce or dressing, I like Hollandaise *28*. **Prep:** Marinate Tempeh *129*.
Monday	**Lunch:** BLT *116* and Black Bean soup (from Sunday's Black Beans). Choose a dressing for the BLT, I like Ranch *27* or Tartar *23*. **Dinner:** Couscous 76. Kill leftover Tempeh Bacon. Choose a sauce, like Zesty Tahini *21,* Curry *50* or Spicy Peanut *42*. **Prep:** Roast a lot of veggies for the next 3 days of the week.
Tuesday	**Lunch:** Salad *100-107*. Choose a dressing, we have suggestions in the Salads section. **Dinner:** Mexican Lasagna *94*, using leftover roasted veggies.
Wednesday	**Lunch:** Roasted Veggies Wrap *122*, using leftover roasted veggies. Choose a sauce or dressing, I like Thousand Island *24*. **Dinner:** Polenta *90* (save trimmings for "fried" polenta for Thursday). Choose a sauce; Tomato *46,* Curry *50* or Mushroom Gravy *44* work great.
Thursday	**Lunch:** Avocado Joy *110* Sandwich and Polenta "Fries" *91*. Choose a sauce or dressing for the wrap, I like Ranch 27*,* Tartar *23* or Ginger Sesame *38* and a dip for the polenta, ketchup will be just fine. **Dinner:** Mushroom Stroganoff *84* over Whole Wheat Pasta. Save some of the Stroganoff for Friday's dinner.
Friday	**Lunch:** Chickpea "Tuna" Salad *120*, sandwich or over greens. **Dinner:** Risotto *71*, using the leftover Mushroom stroganoff as the risotto cream, just adding it to cooked rice.
Saturday	**Lunch:** Roasted Eggplant *140* with whatever leftovers you may still have. Save some roasted eggplant for a sandwich next week. **Dinner:** Salsa and Guacamole *135* with your favorite chips, binge-watching a great show.

Essential shopping lists (plenty for at least 3 people):

These are the essential ingredients you will need for the recipes; we are not including the seasonings, which you probably already have, nor the ingredients for sauces and dressings for your sandwiches, salads, and bowls because we believe it is a matter of personal preference.

Week 1:
3 packs tofu
1 head of broccoli or cauliflower
8 Russet potatoes
5 large tomatoes
6 peppers of various colors
3 large sweet potatoes
1 large zucchini, squash or eggplant
4 large carrots
6-8 large onions
2 large cucumbers (salad, sushi)
Small bag of radishes (salad)
6 avocados (sandwich, salad, sushi)
1 large bag or box of spinach
1 large bag of frozen peas
1 large bag of frozen corn
2 pounds of lentils
2-3 cans chickpeas and or other canned beans of your choice
1 bunch of parsley
1-2 heads of garlic or a bag/case of peeled garlic
Few sprigs of cilantro
1 carton plant milk
1 loaf whole grains bread, or 4-6 large whole-wheat buns
1 pack corn or flour tortillas
2 pounds brown rice
1 pound quinoa
1-2 pounds whole-wheat pasta
1 pound Sushi rice
1 pound raw cashews

Week 2:
1 bag of frozen peas
1 bag of frozen corn
1 head of broccoli or cauliflower
4-6 Russet potatoes
5 large tomatoes
6 peppers of various colors
3 large sweet potatoes
1 large eggplant
4 large carrots
6-8 large onions
2 large cucumbers (salad)
5 avocados (sandwich, salad)
1-2 pounds mushroom (a couple of Portobello caps are welcome)
1 large bag of frozen peas
1 large bag of frozen corn
1 pound black beans
4-8 Banana or Cubanelle peppers
1-2 packs tempeh
1 pound whole-wheat couscous
1-2 pounds brown rice
1 pound polenta
1 pound risotto rice
1-2 pounds whole-wheat pasta
1 pack corn or flour tortillas
2-3 cans chickpeas and or other canned beans of your choice

Basic equipment

Most home kitchens have way more stuff than necessary, cluttering valuable counter and cabinet space. In reality, we use very few items on a daily basis:

Knife: one chef's knife is enough, of good quality, which should feel solid, not wobbly, and razor sharp. Keep it sharp using a honing steel at a 15° angle. Choose a blade between 5" and 9" depending on the size of your hands and your level of comfort; anything larger than that is a sword.

Essential cooking utensils: can opener, scissors, peeler, stirring spoon (wood or high heat plastic for non-stick pans), whisk (silicon for your non-stick pans), serving spoon, high heat spatula, flipping spatula, measuring cups and spoons and a 6" to 12" wide strainer. A funnel can also come in handy to get your dressings into squeeze bottles.

Pots and pans: every time I bought a set, I only used a couple of the pots. For daily use, I just need a 9" to 12" non-stick skillet, a 7" to 8" saucepot, and an 8" to 10" cooking pot. The general rule is that the thicker and heavier, the better, because it better distributes heat, but technology has evolved in distributing heat in thinner pans.

I like nonstick pans, which should never be scrubbed nor go in the dishwasher. There are some concerns about chemicals used in every kind of non-stick cookware, including Teflon™, ceramics, copper and titanium. The American Cancer Society and other regulatory agencies around the world have looked into pans containing Teflon™ and Perfluorooctanoic acid (PFOA) and concluded that it is improbable that the small amounts released onto the air and foods would be sufficient to cause us harm. It is possible. However, that ceramic and titanium coating may eventually prove to be safer choices; I'm afraid that they may not be as non-stick as Teflon™, especially after a few uses, which is very helpful for cooking without oils. Absent of better scientific data, the choice is up to your preference.

Invest in a **slow cooker.** That are models starting at $25; you may go fancier, or just get one with a timer and a low/ high temperature control. This will make it a lot easier to cook beans and rice, and you can have dinner ready when you get home from work.

Pressure cookers like Instant Pot™, work similarly to slow cookers, and also reduce the cooking time. They are very practical.

Cutting board: find a big one, as large as you can store and fit on your counter. Few things in a kitchen are as annoying as a small cutting board.

Blender: no need to go crazy, but good quality does make a difference; it can blend faster and better and can make a greater variety of items, perhaps replacing a food processor. It is difficult to get a cashew cream or a kale smoothie thoroughly blended in a $10 machine.

Coffee maker: some of us still have our vices.

Water spray bottle: This is a handy item to have on the counter: when we roast veggies without oils, either in a pan or in the oven, an occasional spray of water keeps veggies from sticking, drying and burning. Also, spraying bread with a bit of water before reheating them in the oven will bring your loaves back to life, like they are freshly baked.

I do most of my cooking in a **small convection oven**, about 22" x 18". It has a good fan and cooks faster than the stove's oven using less energy. The fan makes a difference; it distributes heat and cooks much better than a small toaster oven. A good model will serve as an air fryer.

Equipment I would dismiss: in addition to the many notoriously useless gadgets like banana slicers and garlic peelers, I would avoid buying anything that takes a lot of counter or storage space and is not used often. Some examples:

- **Juicer:** it's a pain to clean and takes away the pulp fiber; use the blender instead.
- **Bread maker:** unless you are positive you'll be making bread often.
- **Deep fryer:** don't get tempted by the grease.
- **50 knives set:** you'll only use a couple.
- **Food processor:** very useful for large batch cooking at the restaurant, rarely used at home. The blender often replaces it.
- **Mixer:** depends on how much you enjoy baking and how often you realistically will bake desserts and bread or make mashed potatoes.
- **Press grill:** I never use it. You can make panini on your skillet.

Basic techniques

Cutting: Nothing will make you look like a pro like being dexterous with a chef's knife. We encourage you to watch a few of the many instructional videos on YouTube with any French culinary chef demonstrating how to handle a knife: stand at 45 degrees to the cutting board (so your knife will be comfortably at 90 degrees), index and thumb holding the blade, for control, and cut with forward movements, without lifting the knife too far from the cutting board, with the blade touching the intermediate phalanges of the index and middle fingers of the assisting hand, where your fingers are curled. At first, it doesn't feel natural, but it eventually will. Skillful knife techniques will keep you safe and allow you to cut faster and more precisely.

Always **read the entire recipe** before you start. We can't stress this enough: this will allow you to be sure you have all the ingredients and to plan which steps you need to do first.

Recipes are not written in stone: They are guidelines and a good source of ideas. Every person has a different palate for seasoning and ingredients. And often you may not have the exact ingredients in the fridge. **Taste the food as you cook**, play around; use what you have and take notes of what you liked.

Cook in larger batches and **open your mind to leftovers.** Remember Lavoisier: "Nothing is lost, everything is transformed." My wife knows this well: roasted veggies will become a curry, which becomes a different curry and eventually find their way into a fried rice, risotto or pasta.

Always have a sauce and/or dressing made. If you have a dressing, you have a salad. If you have a sauce, you'll save half the time of your meal preparation.

Flavor depth and flavor complexity are fancy ways of saying that our palate enjoys a balance of several flavor components: savory, sweet, tart, bitter, spicy and umami. Meats, for example, are naturally sweet, so we sometimes add a bit of sweetener to meat substitutes. As you season, keep in mind the idea of combining and mixing these several components, as they do so artfully in Asian cuisine.

Season gradually. A friend chef used to tell me that vegetables are subtler than meats; "if you over-season, you don't taste the vegetables anymore". Taste as you cook, play around with your preferred seasonings, but do it in small increments: when you over season something, you can't remove it.

Be smart and efficient: if you are cooking a pasta dish, the first thing you do is boil water. You will have time to gather ingredients and prepare the sauce in the 15 minutes it takes for the water to boil and for the pasta to cook, and then you can get both pasta and sauce done at the same time.

Use fresh herbs and garlic whenever possible. You can bridge this fundamental difference between professional cooking and home cooking. Garlic peals easily by gently pressing the flat side of a chef's knife blade against the clove, and it tastes dramatically better than the jarred. Some supermarkets sell peeled fresh garlic. I buy them, and most restaurants buy them in bulk too.

Soak beans overnight. Dry beans and lentils will cook significantly faster if they soak overnight or for at least 1 hour. I like to add a Tablespoon of garlic powder to the soaking water, to infuse flavor into the beans.

Canned beans and vegetables should be **thoroughly rinsed** before use. The brine in canned garbanzo beans is called *aquafaba* and can be whipped into a meringue consistency. You may save it when draining the garbanzos, to use in a few different recipes as an emulsifier or egg replacement. There are plenty of uses for aquafaba listed online.

Develop the habit of **pre-heating the pan**; I usually turn the heat on while I'm cutting vegetables. It will reduce the sticking of foods to the pan because foods will form a crust as soon as they touch the hot surface. Also, **pre-heat the oven**; it will reduce the cooking time.

As every chef tells his cooks: **clean as you go**. As stuff and dirt accumulates on the counter and sink, the kitchen becomes dysfunctional; you will find yourself out of cutting board, counter or sink space, or looking for a dirty utensil that is at the bottom of the pile, and it is also very frustrating to stare at a collection of dirty pots, utensils, and dishes at the end of the cooking process. While you are waiting for water to boil, or veggies to roast, do some interim cleaning.

Cooking time, flavor, spices, moistness, and consistency will vary. Get comfortable with checking if foods are thoroughly cooked or browned and if seasoning needs adjusting. Different potatoes or types of rice, e.g., will differ considerably in cooking time, and may not match what the recipe tells you. Your sauce will reduce more if your fire is high and will also taste saltier when reduced. No two ovens cook in the same time, even if the temperatures are set the same. Make notes of your findings.

The presentation is relevant, as many parents know; a plate of veggies arranged as a cartoon figure is more likely to be eaten by a child than vegetables randomly arranged. But for the day-to-day cooking, the presentation is quick and casual, as reflected in the pictures of this book.

There are a few good common practices for plating: a) food should stay within the inner rims of the plate or bowl, not spilling over and out. b) garnishing should be edible and should correlate to the remaining ingredients. Sprinkling paprika over the food, for example, is a poor practice, because paprika doesn't taste very good until it is cooked. Same for covering the food with random herbs, which look great, but do not match or complement the taste of the recipe. c) a nice combination of contrasting colors is welcome. d) giving a bit of height and depth can cause a positive impression, because humans are more visually perceptive of verticals than horizontals; this is why chefs tend to group food at the center of the plate and often lean one item on top of the other, as oppose to spreading the components apart on the plate.

Food styling and photography are beautiful forms of art. I have seen food plated so spectacularly that I regretted eating it, and I've seen food stylists and photographers spend 8 hours to capture a single perfect shot of a dish. There are stunning techniques used in food photography, including the fact that the food, as pictured, is often not edible. It may contain hairspray, dyes, stains, wax, and glycerin, or the food may not be fully cooked, so to preserve better color and shape. The perfect shot is not our goal in this book of pragmatic food for daily life. We wanted to present foods here as they will be realistically prepared in home kitchens, and not discourage people by showing presentations that would take hours or just cannot be matched.

Epilogue – The WFPB Journey

My goal with this book is to help people find and stay on the path to a healthier lifestyle, with easy recipes. I hope you enjoy and that your journey will be long and fun!

Let me briefly present our conceptual approach to the Whole Foods Plant-Based – WFPB lifestyle, and clarify some misconceptions.

Whole Foods Plant-Based - WFPB is a lifestyle consisting of eating foods that come from plants, as little processed as possible, as whole as possible, without added oils, using little sugar and little salt. In other words: unrefined and unprocessed foods using whole grains and plants, no animal proteins and fats, including no meats, no eggs, no dairy or any animal derivative products and no extracted oils.

This approach follows the research work of Dr. Campbell as well as many other medical researchers and practitioners, such as Dr. Caldwell B. Esselstyn, Jr., Dr. Neal Barnard, Dr. McDougall, and Dr. Michael Greger, where a broad consensus has formed in that animal proteins, processed foods, oils, and excessive sugar and sodium cause or significantly contribute to many chronic health conditions.

On top of the list are diabetes type 2, heart and coronary diseases and several types of cancer. At the same time, whole foods plant-based diets contribute to the prevention and reversal of such conditions.

Among many excellent books, I strongly encourage you to read Dr. Campbell's "The China Study" and "Whole", as well as Dr. Esselstyn's " Prevent and Reverse Heart Disease", Dr. Neal Barnard's "Program for Reversing Diabetes" and Dr. Michael Greger's "How Not to Die". In very broad lines, the consensual research conclusions are as follows:

Diabetes type 2 is avoidable and mostly caused by dietary choices. The ingestion of processed sugars, refined carbohydrates and animal proteins and, most especially, fats and oils are the primary factors leading to the disease. It is widely accepted that the fat overload in our muscles and liver is the primary driver of insulin resistance in Diabetes 2. A diet of whole plants and complex unrefined carbohydrates, rich in fiber, reduced added sugars and no added oils may significantly improve the clinical condition and even reverse diabetes 2, and allow the return of the pleasure of eating whole grain bread, pasta, rice, potatoes, and fruit.

Cancer growth has been shown in scientific studies to be accelerated in the presence of a diet rich in animal protein, sugar and/or oils. Eliminating these foods may slow the growth of cancer and contribute to cancer remission.

Heart and coronary diseases are often related to inflammation of the arteries, which facilitate the accumulation of plaque, blocking the blood flow and stressing the heart activity. Animal fat and protein, sugar, and oils are leading causes of such inflammation. These foods also interfere with the production of Nitric Oxide, a substance that coats the endothelium, which is the protective lining of the blood vessels. Also, the arteries and veins become more rigid when ingesting these foods, reducing their capability to dilate when more blood flow is required. It is a consensus among coaches that athletes should eat carbohydrates before physical activity; the main reasons being the need for better dilation of the arteries and the fact that animal proteins and fats require significantly more effort to digest. The same principles apply to our daily lives: we feel groggy after a greasy meal and perform much better after a whole foods plant-based fueling.

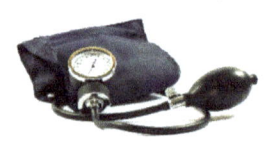

Elevated blood pressure is caused by a variety of factors, including excessive body weight and over-consumption of refined sugars, fat, and sodium. Nutrition is multidimensional and not every person responds in the same manner to nutrients, but the combined reduction of fat, sugar, and sodium has proved to often reduce or even eliminate hypertension. In some cases, going suddenly from a poor diet of fats, high sodium, and empty carbs into a WFPB diet caused a significant and sudden reduction in blood pressure. If your blood pressure is sensitive to changes in diet, you may want to watch your blood pressure diligently, possibly under medical supervision. While the drop in blood pressure is very beneficial in the long run, a sudden drop may bring the danger of fainting. Another upside for people who like me enjoy eating a bit more salt than average, is that a WFPB diet is likely to make your blood pressure a bit more forgiving to sodium.

Fasting has been advocated by some people. I'm not one of them. I have done days-long fasting in my life, and generally felt good about it, but I now believe that I don't need to do it at all. There is not sufficient scientific data to support the benefit of fasting over extended periods. There are clinics in countries such as Germany and Russia that provide medically supervised (crucial) fasting treatment programs of several days, up to 3 weeks. The principles proposed are that the body eliminates food toxins that may contribute to a series of illnesses, such as inflammations, autoimmune diseases, and allergies, and that the digestive system gets a rest and the body has a chance to "reset" and self-heal. It is also proposed that fasting may starve cancers from growing. WFPB doctors generally agree that when following a WFPB lifestyle, fasting, for the purposes listed above, is altogether unnecessary.

Displacement: One issue with eating a diet of animal products, empty carbs, fat sugar, and salt, is the harmful stuff in it. The other factor is that we are not eating the vital nutrients and fiber from the plants, because they are being displaced from the plate by the bad stuff. Except for specific illnesses, hardly anybody in America is deficient in protein, while millions are chronically deficient in fiber, minerals and other micronutrients abundantly found in plants.

Reductionism is a misguided attempt to micromanage our nutrition, opposed by Dr. Campbell and other WFPB researchers. Special interests have long misled us into believing that we need to actively seek to consume specific, precise amounts of nutrients, such as protein, vitamins, minerals, omega 3 fatty acids, etc. In every case, this information has proven to be dubious and often sponsored by the meat, dairy or dietary supplements industries. The truth is that digestion and nutrition are far more complex than any of these presumptuous studies and our current science understands. What do we know, is that foods of animal origin, oils, and excessive sugar and salt contribute to many diseases, and whole foods plant-based contribute to preventing such illnesses.

Recommending that you eat more flavonoid antioxidants is reductionism, and we frankly don't know how effective these nutrients are when consumed isolated from their foods of origin and all other micronutrients that work in synergy, nor how much of them is ideal. What we do know is that people who eat a diverse WFPB diet hardly  ever are found to be deficient in nutrients, except for B12, which is the only recommend supplement. On the other hand, people not on a WFPB are often found to be deficient in a wide variety of nutrients.

To avoid the reductionism trap, the recipes in this book intentionally do not show nutritional values, nor do we make consumption recommendations. We don't suggest you eat flavonoids, we recommend you eat broccoli.

The concepts to have in mind are that it is nearly impossible to be protein-deficient if you are eating enough calories and that when eating WFPB, your body will find its balance. If you are hungry, eat more; if you are a bodybuilder, eat even more. It also takes genuinely eating a lot of food to go overweight when eating WFPB. The guideline is to eat a diverse amount of plants, and it will be improbable that you will be nutritionally unbalanced. If you have a specific condition or deficiency concerns, ask your doctor to address it in your regular blood screenings and consultations, and adjust your diet if necessary.

Just to illustrate the point, here is how much protein can be found in only **one cup** of the following cooked plant-based foods (a person needs an average of 50g per day):

> Lentils: 18g
> Black Beans: 15g
> Chickpeas: 15g
> Quinoa: 9g
> Oats (raw): 26g
> Tofu: 20g
> Brown Rice: 5g

Immune system: Meat, poultry, fish, and dairy are more hospitable to harmful bacteria and viruses than vegetables. When you eat a WFPB diet, you are ingesting fewer pathogens, and you increase the chances of having a stronger and combat-ready immune system when something nasty attacks you from the environment. If you have a condition that weakens your immune system, we suggest that you discuss with your physician the option and benefits of a WFPB diet.

At the same time, the various meat industries generally treat their animals with a generous amount of antibiotics. This has two worrisome and detrimental side-effects: it helps create newer strands of bacteria that are resistant to conventional antibiotics, and these antibiotics cause us to reduce the availability and diversity of friendly bacteria that help our human organism perform various crucial tasks, from digestion to cells replacement. It is estimated that humans, on average, only have now about one third of the gut bacteria diversity than we had 50 years ago. This is one possible reason so many of us suffer from indigestion and constipation, and even certain inflammations as well as some food allergies and intolerance. Most probiotics sold in supermarkets to address this issue only offer a very limited diversity of bacteria.

Evolution of humans is about 300,000 years. By all indications, we were not particularly good hunters, and it took us a while to become good farmers. In the **Paleo**lithic period, we mostly ate fruits, nuts, plants, grains, roots and, occasionally, small animals. Because food was not abundant until the last few decades, our brains adapted to seek the largest amount of calories from scarce sources, hence sugars and fats. Our bodies developed to be omnivore, and take nutrition from whichever source. Evolution hasn't yet factored in the very recent ready availability of veggies in places once too dry, too cold or too hot to sustain any crops. For those who argue that evolution wants us to eat meat, I would offer the thought that evolution doesn't care how healthy you will be in your 90's, only that you reach the age of reproduction.

Confusion: "sometimes I hear that meat, dairy and eggs are good, and sometimes I hear they are bad; it's so confusing!" This is, I'm afraid, intentional and malicious.

For decades, the tobacco industry developed the tactic of confusing the public with technical terminology and funding research leading to conflicting results. The goal was to create a perception that there was no consensus whether smoking was really that bad. The exact same technique is used by the meat, dairy, and processed foods industry.

The fact is that there is no scientific doubt that these foods are unhealthy. While some well-intended people still believe in eating a little of these foods to yield specific necessary nutrients, it's been proven over and over that you can get the same nutrients from healthy plant-based sources.

The only genuine question is the level of tolerance that an individual might have to eating harmful foods without significant consequences.

Perhaps you know someone who lived through her 90's smoking like a chimney. While impressive, there isn't scientific evidence that disproves the facts; it's a statistical gamble. There is no safe cigarette, nor a safe amount of smoking. The same applies to unhealthy foods: one very occasional burger may not kill you; 10 burgers a day, likely will, and we just don't know what level, if any, is safe.

There are a lot of **excellent resources** out there: research and scientific data, social media groups, grassroots activism, new restaurants, and fantastic cookbooks. For special occasions, and as you become more comfortable in the kitchen, there are many excellent books of whole foods plant-based recipes with meals that will astound your family and friends; I would like to recommend the "The PlantPure Nation Cookbook" and "The PlantPure Kitchen" by Kim Campbell. These books feature delicious and still very easy to follow recipes, of which I've tried several, and they have been supervised and approved by Dr. T. Collin Campbell, author of "The China Study" and the world's lead researcher on the health impact of plant-based nutrition vs. the consumption of animal proteins and processed foods. Jane and Ann Esselstyn's "The Prevent and Reverse Heart Disease Cookbook" is also excellent, as is Dr. Michael Greger's "How Not to Die – Cookbook."

Baby Steps

Our goal is to encourage people to start and stay on a better path for a healthier diet. Perhaps you know, as I do, people who are just not yet ready to fully embrace a perfect whole foods plant-based diet. Without being aggressive, pushy or judgmental, here are a few suggestions for encouraging positive incremental change:

Enjoy your food. The meal should be a pleasurable experience, not a punishment. Phase in more veggie stuff you already like, and try to make easy replacements, like whole grains replacing the refined versions of bread, pasta, cereal, chips, and snacks. It makes a huge difference.

Add veggies everywhere. Stuff your sandwich with spinach, tomato, and onions, throw peas in the Mac and Cheese and add all the available veggie toppings to the pizza. Integrate the veggies in the things you like to eat; don't make it a sacrifice to have to eat a side of boring steamed flavorless vegetables.

If a piece of green stuff is scary, blend it into the sauce. The goal is to eat as much as possible of the good, and as little as possible of the bad.

Always have an assortment of vegetables, fresh, frozen and canned so you can do all of the above.

Stick with what you like, with modifications. A simple Portobello is a fantastic replacement for a burger patty in that special burger you love to make with all kinds of fixings.

Use plant milk everywhere you'd use dairy. As Rip Esselstyn likes to say, milk is liquid meat.

Reduce sugary drinks.

Add more veggies and plants to smoothies and juices.

Read labels and choose products that are less processed and have fewer unpronounceable ingredients.

Develop the habit of eating **fruits for dessert and/or breakfast.**

Use a lot less oil than you usually use. Most people can cut down the oils by 3/4ths in their cooking and not even notice the difference.

Replace all white stuff with whole grains. Anybody can get used to whole-wheat pasta, brown rice, and multigrain bread.

Don't start this lifestyle as a diet. Eat until you are satisfied, so that your brain doesn't associate this lifestyle as unpleasant and depriving.

Encourage by example: Dr. Doug Lisle suggest that people don't like to be preached to about their lifestyle; they react better when you just say "I tried this lifestyle, and it's working for me. I'm feeling better than I ever did."

Equivalences

Conventions:
t = tsp = teaspoon   C = Cup
T = Tbsp = Tablespoon   P = Pint
# = lb = Pound   Q = Quart

For Liquids:
1 teaspoon = 1/6 oz
1 Tablespoon = 3 teaspoons = ½ oz
1 oz = 2 Tablespoons
1 Cup = 8 oz = 16 Tablespoons
1 Pint = 2 Cups = 16 oz
1 Quart = 2 Pints = 4 Cups = 32 oz
1 Gallon = 4 Quarts = 8 Pints = 16 Cups = 128 oz

For Powder:
1 teaspoon ≅ 1/12 oz
1 Tablespoon = 3 teaspoons ≅ ¼ oz
1 Cup = 16 Tablespoon ≅ 4 oz
1 Pint = 2 Cups ≅ 8 oz
1 Quart = 2 Pints = 4 Cups ≅ 16 oz
1 Gallon = 4 Quarts = 8 Pints = 16 Cups ≅ 64 oz

Metric:
1 oz ≅ 28 grams
1 Tablespoon ≅ 14 grams
1 pound ≅ 450 grams
1 Kilo ≅ 2.2 Pounds
1 Cup ≅ ¼ liter
1 Pint ≅ ½ liter
1 Galloon ≅ 3.8 liter

So, what can I make, if I have...

ASPARAGUS
Asian Noodle Soups 155 - 157
Breaded Veggie Bites 130
Couscous 76
Creamy Vegetable Soup 142
Crispy Roasted Veggies 140
Enchiladas 92
Everyday Bowl 99
Everyday Salads 100
Fried Rice 66
Gnocchi 98
Last Minute Bowl 78
Pasta 88
Polenta 90
Quiche 162
Risotto 71
Roasted Veggies Wrap 122
Salads 100
Shepherd's Pie 86
Spanish Tortilla 164
Sushi Rolls 69
Tacos 80
Tofu Scramble 160
Veggie Miso Soup 152
Veggies Curry 82

AVOCADO
Ajiaco 144
Chocolate Mousse 141
Everyday Bowl 99
Everyday Salads 100
Everyday Sandwiches 110
Guacamole 137
Last Minute Bowl 78
Roasted Veggies Wrap 122
Sushi Rolls 69
Tacos 80
Veggies Miso Soup 152

BEANS
Bean Burger 116
Black Bean 60
Chili 146
Couscous 76
Enchiladas 92
Everyday Bowl 99
Fried Rice 66
Last Minute Bowl 78
Mexican Lasagna 94
Roasted Veggies Wrap 122
Salsa 135
Shepherd's Pie 86
Stuffed Cabbage 96
Tacos 80

BROCCOLI
Asian Noodle Soups 155 - 157
Breaded Veggie Bites 130
Couscous 76
Creamy Vegetable Soup 142
Crispy Roasted Veggies 140
Enchiladas 92
Everyday Bowl 99
Everyday Salads 100
Fried Rice 66
Gnocchi 98
Last Minute Bowl 78
Pasta 88
Polenta 90
Quiche 162
Risotto 71
Roasted Broccoli 138
Roasted Veggies Wrap 122
Shepherd's Pie 86
Spanish Tortilla 164
Tacos 80
Veggie Miso Soup 152
Veggies Curry 82

Bread
Basic Bread 54
Bean Burger 116
Chickpea Tuna Salad 120
Everyday Sandwiches 110
Tofu Meatballs 126

Cabbage
Asian Noodle Soups 155 - 157
Borscht 148
Couscous 76
Enchiladas 92
Everyday Bowl 99
Everyday Salads 100
Fried Rice 66
Last Minute Bowl 78
Pasta 88
Quiche 162
Roasted Veggies Wrap 122
Stuffed Cabbage 96
Tacos 80

Capers
Caesar 25
Salad 100
Hummus 34
Potato Salad 132
Tabbouleh 103
Tartar 23

Carrot
Asian Noodle Soups 155 - 157
Beans 60
Borscht 148
Breaded Veggie Bites 130
Chili 146
Couscous 76
Creamy Vegetable Soup 142
Crispy Roasted Veggies 140
Enchiladas 92
Everyday Bowl 99
Everyday Salads 100
Fried Rice 66

Ginger Sesame 38
Last Minute Bowl 78
Lentil 62
Pasta 88
Quiche 162
Risotto 71
Roasted Veggies Wrap 122
Shepherd's Pie 86
Spanish Tortilla 164
Sushi 69
Tacos 80
Veggie Miso Soup 152
Veggies Curry 82

Cashews
Cashew Cheese 33
Cashew Cream 30
Creamy Gazpacho 145
Creamy Tomato Sauce 47
Creamy Vegetable Soup 142
Grits 166
Mashed Potatoes 58
Mushroom Gravy 44
Mushroom Stroganoff 84
Potato Salad 132
Red Pepper Coulis 43
Risotto 71

Celery
Asian Noodle Soups 155 - 157
Beans 60
Chickpea Tuna Salad 120
Chili 146
Couscous 76
Creamy Vegetable Soup 142
Enchiladas 92
Everyday Bowl 99
Everyday Salads 100
Everyday Sandwiches 110
Fried Rice 66
Last Minute Bowl 78
Quiche 162
Risotto 71
Roasted Veggies Wrap 122
Salsa 135

Shepherd's Pie 86
Veggies Curry 82
Veggies Miso Soup 152

CHICKPEAS
Burger 116
Chickpea and Spinach 71
Chickpea Tuna Salad 120
Couscous 76
Everyday Bowl 99
Everyday Salads 100
Fried Rice 66
Hummus 34
Last Minute Bowl 78
Shepherd's Pie 86
Veggies Curry 82

COCONUT MILK
Chocolate Mousse 141
Coconut Mushroom Soup 150
Creamy Tomato Sauce 48
Creamy Vegetable Soup 142
Everyday Cereal 160
Gnocchi 98
Grits 166
Mashed Potatoes 58
Mild Curry Sauce 50
Mushroom Stroganoff 84
Potato Salad 132
Risotto 71
Shepherd's Pie 86
Unbelievable Potato Salad 132
Veggies Curry 82
Asian Noodle Soups 155 - 157

CORN
Couscous 76
Creamy Vegetable Soup 142
Enchiladas 92
Everyday Bowl 99
Everyday Salads 100
Fried Rice 66
Last Minute Bowl 78
Lentil 62
Mexican Lasagna 94
Quiche 162
Risotto 71

Roasted Veggies Wrap 122
Salsa 100
Shepherd's Pie 86
Tacos 80
Veggies Curry 82

COUSCOUS
Burger 116
Couscous 76
Everyday Bowl 99
Everyday Salads 100
Last Minute Bowl 78

CUCUMBER
Banh Mi 117
Creamy Gazpacho 145
Everyday Bowl 99
Everyday Salads 100
Everyday Sandwiches 110
Last Minute Bowl 78
Roasted Veggies Wrap 122
Salsa 135
Sushi 69
Tabbouleh 103

EDAMAME
Asian Noodle Soups 155 - 157
Chili 146
Couscous 76
Creamy Vegetable Soup 142
Enchiladas 92
Everyday Bowl 99
Fried Rice 66
Last Minute Bowl 78
Pasta 88
Polenta 90
Potato Scramble 168
Quiche 162

Risotto 71
Shepherd's Pie 86
Spanish Tortilla 164
Stroganoff 84
Tofu Scramble 160

Veggies Curry 82
Veggies Miso Soup 152

EGGPLANT
Bacon 129
Breaded Veggie Bites 130
Couscous 76
Enchiladas 92
Mexican Lasagna 94
Pasta Primavera 88
Quiche 162
Roasted Eggplant 140
Roasted Veggies Wrap 122
Sandwiches 110
Shepherd's Pie 86
Tacos 80
Tofu Scramble 160
Veggies Curry 82
Veggies Miso Soup 152

FLOUR
Bread 54
Breaded Veggie Bites 130
Crispy Roasted Veggies 140
Pancakes 170

GRITS
Arepas 159
Grits 166
Polenta 90

KALE
Chickpea and Spinach 71
Couscous 76
Creamy Vegetable Soup 142
Enchiladas 92
Everyday Bowl 99
Everyday Salads 100
Everyday Sandwiches 110
Fried Rice 66
Last Minute Bowl 78
Mexican Lasagna 94

Pasta 88
Polenta 90
Quiche 162
Risotto 71
Shepherd's Pie 86
Spanish Tortilla 164
Stuffed Leaves 96
Tabbouleh 103
Tacos 80
Veggies Curry 82

LENTIL
Lentils 62
Shepherds Pie 86
Burger 116

MISO
Asian Noodle Soups 155 - 157
Caesar 25
Veggies Miso Soup 152

MUSHROOM
Asian Noodle Soups 155 - 157
Bacon 129
Breaded Veggie Bites 130
Brown Sauce (Gravy) 39
Chili 146
Couscous 76
Creamy Vegetable Soup 142
Crispy Roasted Veggies 140
Enchiladas 92
Everyday Bowl 99
Everyday Sandwiches 110
Fried Rice 66
Last Minute Bowl 78
Mexican Lasagna 94
Mushroom Gravy 44
Pasta 88
Polenta 90
Potato Scramble 168
Quiche 162
Risotto 71
Roasted Veggies Wrap 122
Shepherd's Pie 86

Spanish Tortilla 164
Stroganoff 84
Tacos 80
Tofu Scramble 160
Veggies Curry 82
Veggies Miso Soup 152

OLIVES
Caesar 25
Chickpea Tuna Salad 120
Hummus 34
Potato Salad 132
Tabbouleh 103
Tartar 23

ONION
Asian Noodle Soups 155 - 157
Beans 60
Breaded Veggie Bites 130
Brown Sauce (Gravy) 39
Caesar 25
Chickpea Tuna Salad 120
Chili 146
Couscous 76
Crispy Roasted Veggies 140
Enchiladas 92
Everyday Bowl 99
Everyday Salads 100
Everyday Sandwiches 110
Fried Rice 66
Last Minute Bowl 78
Lentil 62
Mexican Lasagna 94
Mushroom Gravy 44
Pasta 88
Polenta 90
Potato Salad 132
Potato Scramble 168
Quiche 162
Risotto 71
Roasted Veggies Wrap 122
Salsa 135
Shepherd's Pie 86
Spanish Tortilla 164

Stroganoff 84
Tacos 80
Tofu Scramble 160
Veggies Curry 82
Veggies Miso Soup 152

PARSLEY
Balsamic Vinaigrette 36
Tabbouleh 103
Unbelievable Potato Salad 132

PASTA
Asian Noodle Soups 155 - 157
Burger 116
Pasta Alfredo 32
Pasta Primavera 88
Pesto Pasta 107
Spanish Tortilla 164
Stroganoff 84
Tofu Meatball 126
Tofu Meatloaf 127
Veggies Miso Soup 152

PEAS
Asian Noodle Soups 155 - 157
Chili 146
Couscous 76
Creamy Vegetable Soup 142
Enchiladas 92
Everyday Bowl 99
Fried Rice 66
Last Minute Bowl 78
Pasta 88
Polenta 90
Potato Scramble 168
Quiche 162
Risotto 71
Shepherd's Pie 86
Spanish Tortilla 164
Stroganoff 84
Tofu Scramble 160
Veggies Curry 82
Veggies Miso Soup 152

Peanut or Peanut Butter
Curry Sauce 50
PB&J (recipe is in the name)
Spicy Peanut Sauce 42
Zesty Tahini 21

Peppers
Asian Noodle Soups 155 - 157
Beans 60
Breaded Veggie Bites 130
Chili 146
Couscous 76
Creamy Gazpacho 145
Creamy Vegetable Soup 142
Crispy Roasted Veggies 140
Enchiladas 92
Everyday Bowl 99
Everyday Salads 100
Everyday Sandwiches 110
Fried Rice 66
Last Minute Bowl 78
Mexican Lasagna 94
Pasta 88
Polenta 90
Potato Scramble 168
Quiche 162
Red Pepper Coulis 43
Risotto 71
Roasted Veggies Wrap 122
Salsa 135
Shepherd's Pie 86
Spanish Tortilla 164
Tacos 80
Tofu Scramble 160
Veggies Curry 82
Veggies Miso Soup 152

Pickles
Banh Mi 117
Burger 116
Everyday Sandwiches 110
Tartar 23
Thousand Island 24

Polenta
Arepas 159
Grits 166
Polenta 90
Polenta "Fries" 91

Potato
Ajiaco 144
Asian Noodle Soups 155 - 157
Chili 146
Couscous 76
Enchiladas 92
Everyday Bowl 99
Latkes 134
Leek and Potato Soup 144
Lentils 62
Mashed Potatoes 58
Potato Salad 132
Potato Scramble 168
Shepherd's Pie 86
Spanish Tortilla 164
Veggies Curry 82
Veggies Miso Soup 152

Rice
Basic Rice 55
Burger 116
Everyday Bowl 99
Fried Rice 66
Last Minute Bowl 78
Risotto 71
Stuffed Cabbage 96
Stuffed Peppers 134
Sushi 68
Tofu Meatball 126
Tofu Meatloaf 127

Spinach
Chickpea and Spinach 71
Couscous 76
Creamy Vegetable Soup 142
Enchiladas 92
Everyday Bowl 99

Everyday Salads 100
Everyday Sandwiches 110
Fried Rice 66
Last Minute Bowl 78
Mexican Lasagna 94
Pasta 88
Polenta 90
Quiche 162
Risotto 71
Roasted Veggies Wrap 122
Shepherd's Pie 86
Spanish Tortilla 164
Tabbouleh 103
Tacos 80
Tofu Scramble 160
Veggies Curry 82

Sweet Potato
Breaded Veggie Bites 130
Couscous 76
Creamy Vegetable Soup 142
Crispy Roasted Veggies 140
Enchiladas 92
Everyday Bowl 99
Everyday Salads 100
Everyday Sandwiches 110
Fried Rice 66
Last Minute Bowl 78
Mexican Lasagna 94
Risotto 71
Roasted Veggies Wrap 122
Shepherd's Pie 86
Spanish Tortilla 164
Tacos 80
Tofu Scramble 160
Veggies Curry 82

Tahini
Creamy Tomato Sauce 47
Ginger Sesame 38
Hummus 34
Zesty Tahini 21

Tortilla & wraps
Burger 116

Mexican Lasagna 94
Tofu Meatball 126
Tofu Meatloaf 127
Wraps 110

Tomato
Beans 60
Chili 146
Couscous 76
Creamy Gazpacho 145
Creamy Tomato Sauce 47
Creamy Vegetable Soup 142
Enchiladas 92
Everyday Bowl 99
Everyday Salads 100
Everyday Sandwiches 110
Fried Rice 66
Last Minute Bowl 78
Mexican Lasagna 94
Pasta 88
Polenta 90
Quiche 162
Roasted Veggies Wrap 122
Salsa 135
Shepherd's Pie 86
Tabbouleh 103
Tacos 80
Tomato Sauce 46

Tofu
Asian Noodle Soups 155 - 157
Baked Tofu 125
Caesar 25
Chocolate Mousse 141
Cilantro 26
Curry Mayo 41
Easy Banh Mi 117
Egg Salad 107
Everyday Bowl 99
Everyday Salads 100
Everyday Sandwiches 110
Fried Rice 66
Last Minute Bowl 78
Mayo 22

Mexican Lasagna 94
Quiche 162
Quick Hollandaise 28
Ranch 155
Roasted Veggies Wrap 122
Spanish Tortilla 164
Tartar 23
Thousand Island 24
Tofu Meatball 126
Tofu Meatloaf 127
Tofu Scramble 160

ZUCCHINI
Asian Noodle Soups 155 - 157
Breaded Veggie Bites 130
Couscous 76

Crispy Roasted Veggies 140
Enchiladas 92
Everyday Bowl 99
Everyday Salads 100
Everyday Sandwiches 110
Fried Rice 66
Mexican Lasagna 94
Quiche 162
Risotto 71
Shepherd's Pie 86
Spanish Tortilla 164
Tofu Scramble 160
Veggies Curry 82
Veggies Miso Soup 152
Roasted Veggies Wrap 122
Zucchini Bread 54

Acknowledgements and Credits

My wife, for the support and dedication to the principle of a plant-based lifestyle and the many contributions to this book.

All the clients and friends at Vge Café and PlantPure Café for all the support and love over the years, and for compelling me to write this book.

Nelson and Kim Campbell, for the friendship, support, and mentorship.

Dr. T. Colin Campbell, whose life's work blazed the trail for all of us in the plant-based movement.

Sheryl Riddell, for the help with this book and all the support over the years.

Charlene Nolan for the guidance, mentorship, and support from the day I first opened Vge Café.

All of the Animal welfare organizations, rescues, environmental groups, scientific searchers, plant-based advocates and everyone promoting, supporting and enjoying this lifestyle, thank you for making the world better.

Pictures not by the Author:

Fresh Vegetables, Lotus_studio/shutterstock
Mushrooms, Engin_Akyurt/pixabay
Food, HG-Fotografie/pixabay
Electric Blender, ProstoSvet/shutterstock
Avocado, Icb/pixabay
Cilantro, tlarussa/pixabay
Mixed Vegetables, Alexandra Lande/shutterstock
Cinnamon, ulleo/pixabay
Zucchini Soup, etorres/shutterstock
Cashews, Giovanni42/pixabay
Kale, azboomer/pixabay
Tofu, yuelanliu/pixabay
Wheat, hzcf428526/pixabay
Different oils, yamix/shutterstock
Tomatoes, hansbenn/pixabay
Glass of wine, maciej326/pixabay
Vegetables basket, congerdesign/pixabay
Asparagus, ritae/pixabay
egetarian dish made of kidney bean, Ildi Papp/shutterstock
Healthy vegetable salad, sea wave/shutterstock
Fusilli pasta, Elenadesign/shutterstock
Salad, stock snap/pixabay
Cutting Board, stock snap/pixabay
Eggplant, I_hoernchen-2551412/pixabay
Palm Tree, Alfonso2873/pixabay
Udon, KoalaParkLaundromat/pixabay
Market, PhotoMIX-Company/pixabay
Spices, Sommerwolke/pixabay
GMO, artursfoto/pixabay
Germ, SarahRichterArt/pixabay
Knife, SteveRaubenstine/pixabay
Sphygmomanometer, frolicsomepl/pixabay
Red pepper, AliceKeyStudio/pixabay
Tomato soup, catkin/pixabay
Tomato sauce, tjena/pixabay
Cooking Pot, OpenClipart-Vectors/pixabay
Cooking Pan, OpenClipart-Vectors/pixabay
Blender, OpenClipart-Vectors/pixabay
Knife, OpenClipart-Vectors/pixabay
Stove, anarosadebastiani/pixabay
Stopwatch, OpenClipart-Vectors/pixabay
Tube measure, Clker-Free-Vector-Images/pixabay
Scale, OpenClipart-Vectors/pixabay
Frying pan, thegiwi/pixabay
Fresh Salad, Anna_Pustynnikova/shutterstock
Cauliflower, Nate Allred/shutterstock
Mashed Potatoes, Africa Studio/shutterstock
Healthy Salad, Elena Veselova/shutterstock
Gazpacho, nesavinov/shutterstock
Beetroot soup, Food Photography for Biz/shutterstock
Haomade gravy, Elena Veselova/shutterstock
Broccoli, Engin_Akyurt/pixabay
Measuring cup, Monfocus/pixabay
Leek Soup, HandmadePictures/shutterstock
Sandwich with tomato sauce, Igor Dutina/shutterstock
Mushroom Sandwich, Ezume Images/shutterstock
Caesar, dronG/Shutterstock
macandcheese, Tacar/shutterstock
pasta with creamy sauce, travellight/shutterstock
hollandaise, Peter Hermes Furian/shutterstock
veggies sandwich, Mi.Ti./shuterstock
Vegetables, HG-Fotografie/pixabay